The Power of Self-Disciplin
Your Habits and Mindset

Hawkin

Copyright © [2023]

Title: The Power of Self-Discipline: Transforming Your Habits and Mindset
Author's: Hawkin

This book was printed and published by [Publisher's: **Hawkin**] in [2023]

ISBN:

TABLE OF CONTENT

Chapter 3: Building a Foundation for Self-Discipline 24

Chapter 4: Developing Self-Discipline in Daily Life 32

Chapter 5: Strengthening Self-Discipline in Relationships 40

Chapter 9: Empowering Your Life with Self-Discipline   121

Improving Personal and Professional Relationships

Enhancing Productivity and Time Management Skills

Achieving Personal Goals and Ambitions

Cultivating Happiness and Fulfillment

Chapter 10: Maintaining Self-Discipline Beyond the Book   44

Integrating Self-Discipline into Daily Life

Seeking Continuous Growth and Development

Joining Supportive Communities and Networks

Inspiring Others through Your Self-Discipline Journey

Chapter 1: Understanding Self-Discipline

The Importance of Self-Discipline

Self-discipline is the key to unlocking your true potential and achieving success in all aspects of life. It is the ability to control your thoughts, emotions, and actions in order to make positive choices that align with your goals and values. In the book "The Power of Self-Discipline: Transforming Your Habits and Mindset," we delve into the significance of self-discipline and how it can transform your life.

For everyone, regardless of their background or aspirations, self-discipline is crucial. It is the foundation upon which all other personal development efforts are built. Without self-discipline, it is challenging to stay focused, motivated, and committed to achieving your goals. It is the driving force that propels you forward, even when faced with obstacles and setbacks.

In the subchapter, "The Importance of Self-Discipline," we explore the profound impact it has on various areas of your life. From your physical health and fitness to your relationships, career, and personal growth, self-discipline plays a vital role in shaping your outcomes. It enables you to make informed choices and resist temptations that may hinder your progress.

Furthermore, self-discipline empowers you to develop healthy habits and routines that contribute to your overall well-being. It helps you prioritize your time and energy, ensuring that you allocate resources towards activities that align with your long-term goals. With self-discipline, you are less likely to succumb to procrastination or be swayed by short-term gratification, allowing you to achieve greater success and fulfillment.

In this subchapter, we also explore strategies and techniques to cultivate self-discipline. From creating a clear vision and setting SMART goals to implementing effective time management and practicing self-control, we provide practical advice to help you strengthen your self-discipline muscle.

"The Importance of Self-Discipline" is not just about self-control or restraint; it is about taking charge of your life and becoming the best version of yourself. It is about embracing the power to choose your actions and thoughts consciously. With self-discipline, you can overcome challenges, break free from limiting beliefs, and create a life of purpose and meaning.

Whether you are seeking personal growth, professional success, or improved relationships, self-discipline is the key that unlocks the door to your full potential. By cultivating self-discipline, you embark on a transformative journey towards a life of achievement, fulfillment, and lasting happiness.

The Benefits of Developing Self-Discipline

In today's fast-paced world, self-discipline has become an essential trait for success and personal growth. It is the ability to control your thoughts, emotions, and actions in order to achieve your goals and lead a fulfilling life. Developing self-discipline is not an easy task, but the rewards it brings are truly life-changing. In this subchapter, we will explore the numerous benefits of cultivating self-discipline and why it is crucial for everyone.

One of the primary benefits of self-discipline is the ability to overcome procrastination. We all have tasks and responsibilities that we tend to put off, but with self-discipline, we can break free from this habit. By developing a routine and executing tasks promptly, we become more productive and accomplish more in less time. This increased efficiency leads to a sense of accomplishment and boosts our self-confidence.

Furthermore, self-discipline enables us to make better choices and resist instant gratification. It helps us stick to our long-term goals rather than succumbing to short-term temptations. By delaying gratification and practicing self-control, we develop a stronger willpower that allows us to make healthier lifestyle choices, such as exercising regularly, eating nutritious foods, and avoiding harmful habits.

Another significant benefit of self-discipline is improved mental and emotional well-being. When we have control over our thoughts and emotions, we can handle stressful situations more effectively. Self-discipline helps us develop resilience, enabling us to bounce back from setbacks and maintain a positive attitude. It also promotes mindfulness and self-awareness, which are essential for managing stress and achieving inner peace.

Moreover, self-discipline plays a crucial role in building strong relationships. It helps us become more reliable, responsible, and accountable individuals, which are all qualities that people appreciate in their interactions. By practicing self-discipline, we not only enhance our own lives but also positively impact the lives of those around us.

In conclusion, developing self-discipline is a transformative journey that brings numerous benefits to our personal and professional lives. It allows us to overcome procrastination, make better choices, improve mental and emotional well-being, and build strong relationships. The power of self-discipline lies in its ability to shape our habits and mindset, propelling us towards success and fulfillment. So, embrace self-discipline and unlock your true potential!

Differentiating Self-Discipline from Willpower

In our pursuit of personal growth and success, the terms self-discipline and willpower are often used interchangeably. While they are closely related, understanding the subtle differences between the two can have a profound impact on our ability to transform our habits and mindset. In this subchapter, we will delve into the nuances of self-discipline and willpower, and how they can each contribute to our journey towards achieving our goals.

Self-discipline can be defined as the ability to control one's impulses, desires, and actions in order to achieve a specific outcome or objective. It is the internal compass that guides us towards making consistent choices that align with our long-term goals. Self-discipline is a learned behavior, cultivated through practice and repetition. It requires setting clear boundaries, prioritizing tasks, and developing a strong sense of determination and perseverance.

Willpower, on the other hand, is the mental strength and resolve to resist short-term temptations or distractions. It is the force that enables us to overcome momentary desires and stay focused on our long-term objectives. Willpower is like a muscle that can be strengthened through regular exercise. However, it is a finite resource that can be depleted over time, especially when faced with decision fatigue or stressful situations.

While self-discipline and willpower are interconnected, self-discipline is the foundation upon which willpower thrives. Self-discipline provides the structure and routine necessary to minimize the need for constant decision-making, thus conserving willpower for critical moments. By incorporating self-discipline into our daily lives, we create an environment that supports our long-term goals, making it easier to withstand the allure of instant gratification.

Developing self-discipline requires self-awareness, commitment, and a growth mindset. It involves breaking down larger goals into smaller, manageable tasks, and consistently taking action towards their achievement. By establishing healthy habits and routines, we create a framework that reduces the reliance on willpower alone. Self-discipline becomes an ingrained part of our lifestyle, making it easier to resist distractions and temptations.

In conclusion, self-discipline and willpower are two sides of the same coin, each playing a vital role in our pursuit of personal and professional success. By understanding and harnessing the power of self-discipline, we can cultivate the mental strength and resilience needed to overcome obstacles and transform our habits and mindset. So, let us embark on this journey together, embracing self-discipline as our guiding light towards a more fulfilled and purposeful life.

Myths and Misconceptions about Self-Discipline

Self-discipline is a powerful tool that can transform your habits and mindset, allowing you to achieve your goals and live a more fulfilling life. However, there are several myths and misconceptions surrounding self-discipline that can hinder your progress and prevent you from harnessing its true potential. In this subchapter, we will debunk these myths and shed light on the truth behind self-discipline.

Myth 1: Self-discipline is only for a select few
One common misconception is that self-discipline is a trait possessed only by a few individuals who are naturally driven and motivated. However, self-discipline is a skill that can be developed and honed by anyone. It is not an innate quality but a choice we make daily to prioritize our goals and take consistent action towards them. With the right mindset and strategies, anyone can cultivate self-discipline and reap its benefits.

Myth 2: Self-discipline is about deprivation
Another myth about self-discipline is that it requires constant sacrifice and deprivation. While it does involve making disciplined choices and resisting instant gratification, it is not solely about denying yourself pleasure. True self-discipline is about finding a balance between short-term desires and long-term goals. It is about making conscious decisions that align with your values and priorities, allowing you to enjoy both present pleasures and future rewards.

Myth 3: Self-discipline means being rigid and inflexible
Many people believe that self-discipline involves strict rules and rigidity, leaving no room for spontaneity or enjoyment. However, self-

discipline is not about being rigid; it is about being adaptable and resilient. It is about staying focused on your goals while being open to adjusting your plans and strategies as needed. Self-discipline empowers you to make intentional choices and adapt to changing circumstances, ensuring your progress and success.

Myth 4: Self-discipline is a one-time achievement Some individuals perceive self-discipline as a one-time accomplishment, assuming that once you achieve it, you no longer have to work on it. However, self-discipline is a lifelong journey that requires consistent effort and practice. It is a muscle that needs to be exercised regularly to stay strong. By cultivating self-discipline as a habit, you create a positive cycle of success, where discipline becomes second nature and propels you towards your goals effortlessly.

In conclusion, self-discipline is not limited to a select few, nor is it about deprivation or rigidity. It is a skill that can be developed by anyone, allowing you to find balance, adaptability, and lifelong growth. By debunking these myths and embracing the truth about self-discipline, you can harness its power to transform your habits and mindset, unlocking your full potential and achieving the success you desire.

Chapter 2: Assessing Your Current Habits and Mindset

Recognizing Your Strengths and Weaknesses

Self-discipline is a vital trait that can propel us towards achieving our goals and transforming our lives. However, before we embark on this journey, it is crucial to take a step back and truly understand ourselves. This subchapter titled "Recognizing Your Strengths and Weaknesses" delves into the importance of introspection and self-awareness in building self-discipline.

Understanding our strengths and weaknesses allows us to leverage our abilities and address areas that require improvement. Each one of us possesses unique talents and qualities that can be harnessed to maximize our potential. By recognizing our strengths, we can focus our efforts on areas where we excel, increasing our chances of success. Whether it's exceptional organizational skills, effective communication, or creative problem-solving, acknowledging these strengths provides a solid foundation for self-discipline.

On the other hand, identifying our weaknesses is equally important. Self-discipline requires us to be honest with ourselves and face our shortcomings head-on. It is through this awareness that we can develop strategies to overcome obstacles and turn our weaknesses into strengths. Whether it's procrastination, lack of focus, or poor time management, recognizing these weaknesses empowers us to take proactive steps towards improvement.

Recognizing both our strengths and weaknesses also helps us set realistic goals. By understanding our capabilities, we can establish objectives that challenge us without overwhelming us. This self-awareness prevents us from setting unattainable goals that may lead to frustration and a lack of motivation. Instead, we can set achievable targets that stretch our abilities while still being within our reach, ensuring a continuous cycle of growth and progress.

Moreover, recognizing our strengths and weaknesses fosters self-acceptance and self-compassion. We understand that we are not perfect and that it is okay to make mistakes. Instead of dwelling on our weaknesses, we can focus on self-improvement and personal growth. This positive mindset is crucial in maintaining self-discipline, as it allows us to bounce back from setbacks and persevere through challenges.

In conclusion, recognizing our strengths and weaknesses is a fundamental aspect of building self-discipline. It provides us with a solid foundation for growth and empowers us to set realistic goals. By embracing our strengths and addressing our weaknesses, we can embark on a transformative journey towards self-improvement and success. Remember, self-discipline is not about being perfect; it's about understanding ourselves and continuously striving to become the best version of ourselves.

Identifying Habits that Hinder Self-Discipline

Chapter 3: Identifying Habits that Hinder Self-Discipline

Introduction:

In our quest to develop self-discipline, it is crucial to identify the habits that hinder our progress. These habits act as roadblocks, preventing us from reaching our goals and living a fulfilling life. In this subchapter, we will delve into the common habits that hinder self-discipline, and learn how to overcome them.

1. Procrastination:

Procrastination is the enemy of self-discipline. It is the habit of delaying tasks or activities that require our attention. Whether it's putting off that important project, avoiding exercise, or postponing important decisions, procrastination weakens our self-discipline. By recognizing our tendency to procrastinate and developing strategies to combat it, we can regain control over our actions and increase our productivity.

2. Lack of Focus:

In today's fast-paced world, distractions are everywhere. From social media notifications to constant interruptions, our ability to focus is constantly challenged. Lack of focus hampers self-discipline as it diverts our attention away from our goals and prevents us from completing tasks efficiently. By practicing mindfulness, prioritizing tasks, and creating a distraction-free environment, we can strengthen our focus and enhance our self-discipline.

3. Negative Self-Talk:

Our inner dialogue plays a significant role in shaping our behavior and actions. Negative self-talk, such as self-doubt, self-criticism, and self-limiting beliefs, can erode our self-discipline. It diminishes our confidence and hinders progress. By cultivating a positive mindset, practicing self-compassion, and challenging negative thoughts, we can overcome this habit and empower ourselves to pursue our goals with determination.

4. Lack of Planning and Organization:

Without a clear plan and organization, it is easy to lose track of our objectives and succumb to chaos. Disorganization creates unnecessary stress, leading to a lack of motivation and self-discipline. By setting clear goals, creating schedules, and organizing our environment, we can establish a structured framework that supports self-discipline and facilitates success.

Conclusion:

Identifying the habits that hinder self-discipline is a crucial step towards personal growth and transformation. By addressing procrastination, lack of focus, negative self-talk, and lack of planning and organization, we can overcome the obstacles that stand in our way. With self-awareness and determination, we can cultivate habits that foster self-discipline, leading us towards a more fulfilling and successful life.

Remember, self-discipline is not an innate trait but a skill that can be developed and strengthened over time. By understanding the habits that hinder our progress, we can take proactive steps to overcome them and unlock our true potential. So, let us embark on this journey of self-discovery and transformation, one habit at a time.

Assessing Your Mindset and Beliefs

In the journey towards self-discipline, one crucial aspect that often goes unnoticed is assessing your mindset and beliefs. Our mindset plays a significant role in shaping our habits, actions, and ultimately our success. The power of self-discipline lies not only in transforming our habits but also in rewiring our minds for success.

To begin this transformative journey, it is essential to take a step back and evaluate your current mindset and beliefs. Our mindset can be broadly categorized into two types: a fixed mindset and a growth mindset. A fixed mindset believes that our abilities and qualities are fixed traits that cannot be changed. On the other hand, a growth mindset recognizes that we have the potential to learn, grow, and improve with effort and dedication.

Assessing your mindset is crucial because it determines how you approach challenges, setbacks, and even accomplishments. A fixed mindset often leads to a fear of failure and a resistance to taking risks, as individuals believe that failure defines their worth. A growth mindset, however, embraces challenges as opportunities for growth and views failure as a stepping stone towards success.

Beliefs also play a significant role in shaping our mindset. Our beliefs are formed through our experiences, upbringing, and societal influences. It is important to identify and evaluate the beliefs that may be holding you back from achieving self-discipline. For example, if you believe that you are inherently lazy or lacking willpower, it becomes a self-fulfilling prophecy. By challenging these negative beliefs and replacing them with empowering ones, you can unlock your true potential.

Assessing your mindset and beliefs requires self-reflection and introspection. Take the time to ask yourself critical questions: What beliefs do I hold about myself and my abilities? Are these beliefs limiting or empowering? How do I approach challenges and setbacks? Am I open to learning and growth?

Once you have identified any limiting beliefs or a fixed mindset, the next step is to replace them with empowering beliefs and cultivate a growth mindset. This can be achieved through affirmations, positive self-talk, and consciously challenging negative thoughts. Surrounding yourself with like-minded individuals who embody a growth mindset can also be immensely beneficial.

Remember, self-discipline begins with the mind. By assessing your mindset and beliefs, you lay the foundation for personal transformation. Embracing a growth mindset and empowering beliefs will enable you to overcome obstacles, develop new habits, and ultimately achieve the self-discipline you desire.

Strategies for Self-Reflection and Evaluation

Self-reflection and evaluation are vital components of personal growth and self-discipline. They allow us to gain insight into our thoughts, emotions, and behaviors, helping us identify areas for improvement and make positive changes in our lives. In this subchapter, we will explore effective strategies for self-reflection and evaluation to enhance your self-discipline and transform your habits and mindset.

1. Journaling: Keeping a journal is a powerful tool for self-reflection. Take a few minutes each day to write down your thoughts, experiences, and goals. Reflect on your successes and challenges, and identify patterns or triggers that may be hindering your progress. Journaling provides a safe space for introspection and helps you gain clarity and perspective.

2. Mindfulness: Practicing mindfulness involves being fully present in the moment and non-judgmentally observing your thoughts and emotions. By cultivating this awareness, you can identify negative thought patterns or self-sabotaging behaviors that hinder your self-discipline. Mindfulness also helps you develop a sense of calm and focus, enabling you to make more intentional choices.

3. Seeking feedback: Feedback from trusted individuals can provide valuable insights for self-reflection. Reach out to mentors, friends, or family members who can offer constructive criticism and guidance. This feedback can help identify blind spots and offer new perspectives, leading to personal growth and increased self-discipline.

4. Goal setting and tracking: Set clear and measurable goals for yourself, both short-term and long-term. Regularly evaluate your

progress towards these goals and adjust your strategies accordingly. Tracking your progress helps you stay accountable and motivated, while also providing opportunities for self-reflection and evaluation.

5. Analyzing past failures: Instead of dwelling on past failures, use them as learning opportunities. Analyze what went wrong and identify the factors that contributed to the failure. This exercise helps you understand your weaknesses and develop strategies to overcome them, fostering self-discipline and resilience.

6. Celebrating successes: Acknowledge and celebrate your achievements, no matter how small. Recognizing your progress boosts motivation and self-confidence, reinforcing your self-discipline. Take time to reflect on what worked well and replicate those strategies in other areas of your life.

By implementing these strategies, you can cultivate self-discipline and transform your habits and mindset. Self-reflection and evaluation are ongoing processes that require patience and commitment. Embrace these practices as part of your journey towards personal growth and self-mastery. Remember, self-discipline is a skill that can be developed and strengthened with consistent effort and self-reflection.

Chapter 3: Building a Foundation for Self-Discipline

Setting Clear and Meaningful Goals

In the journey towards self-discipline, one of the most crucial aspects is setting clear and meaningful goals. Without proper goals, we may find ourselves wandering aimlessly, lacking direction and motivation. By setting clear and meaningful goals, we can harness the power of self-discipline and transform our habits and mindset.

To begin with, clear goals provide us with a roadmap for success. They allow us to define what we want to achieve and create a plan to get there. Without a clear goal in mind, we may find ourselves scattered and unfocused, wasting time and energy on activities that do not align with our true desires. By setting clear goals, we can prioritize our efforts and work towards achieving what truly matters to us.

Furthermore, meaningful goals give us a sense of purpose and fulfillment. When we set goals that are aligned with our values and passions, we tap into our intrinsic motivation. We become driven by a deep sense of purpose, which fuels our self-discipline and keeps us committed even in the face of challenges. Meaningful goals provide us with a sense of direction and give our actions a greater sense of purpose.

In order to set clear and meaningful goals, it is important to follow a few key steps. First, take the time to reflect on your values and passions. What truly matters to you? What are your long-term aspirations? By understanding your core values and passions, you can set goals that are in alignment with who you are and what you want to achieve.

Next, make your goals specific and measurable. Rather than setting vague goals like "lose weight" or "save money," define exactly what you want to achieve and set a measurable target. For example, "lose 10 pounds in three months" or "save $500 per month." Specific and measurable goals allow you to track your progress and stay accountable.

Additionally, break your goals down into smaller, manageable steps. By breaking a big goal into smaller milestones, you can make your journey more achievable and less overwhelming. Celebrate your progress along the way, as this will boost your motivation and reinforce your self-discipline.

In conclusion, setting clear and meaningful goals is a fundamental aspect of self-discipline. By defining what we want to achieve, aligning our goals with our values, and breaking them down into smaller steps, we can unleash the power of self-discipline and transform our habits and mindset. Remember, the key is to set goals that truly matter to you and provide a sense of purpose and fulfillment. With clear and meaningful goals, you can become the master of your own destiny and achieve remarkable success in all areas of your life.

Creating a Personalized Action Plan

In order to transform our habits and mindset, it is crucial to have a personalized action plan. This plan will serve as a roadmap to guide us through the journey of self-discipline and help us achieve our goals. By following a well-designed action plan, we can effectively harness the power of self-discipline and make lasting changes in our lives.

The first step in creating a personalized action plan is to clearly define our goals. What is it that we want to achieve? Whether it is improving our health, advancing in our career, or cultivating meaningful relationships, it is essential to have a specific and measurable goal in mind. This will allow us to focus our efforts and track our progress along the way.

Once we have identified our goals, the next step is to break them down into smaller, manageable tasks. This will prevent us from feeling overwhelmed and increase our chances of success. Each task should be realistic and have a clear deadline associated with it. By breaking down our goals into smaller steps, we can tackle them one at a time and steadily make progress.

After outlining the tasks, it is important to prioritize them based on their importance and urgency. By doing so, we can allocate our time and energy more effectively. It is also helpful to consider any potential obstacles or challenges that may arise and develop strategies to overcome them. This proactive approach will ensure that we stay on track and are prepared for any setbacks that may come our way.

In addition to prioritizing tasks, it is crucial to establish a routine that supports our goals. This includes setting aside dedicated time each day or week to work on our action plan. By incorporating our tasks into our daily or weekly schedule, we are more likely to stick to them and make progress. It is also important to create a conducive environment that minimizes distractions and promotes focus.

Lastly, regularly reviewing and adjusting our action plan is essential for long-term success. As we progress towards our goals, our priorities or circumstances may change. By regularly assessing our plan, we can make necessary adjustments and stay aligned with our evolving aspirations.

Creating a personalized action plan is a powerful tool for cultivating self-discipline. By defining our goals, breaking them down into manageable tasks, prioritizing, establishing routines, and reviewing our plan regularly, we can harness the power of self-discipline and transform our habits and mindset. Remember, self-discipline is a journey, and with a personalized action plan, we can pave the way towards a more fulfilling and successful life.

Cultivating a Growth Mindset

In the journey of personal development and self-discipline, one of the most powerful tools you can possess is a growth mindset. This outlook on life allows you to embrace challenges, persist in the face of setbacks, and ultimately achieve your goals. By understanding and adopting a growth mindset, you can transform your habits and mindset, unlocking your full potential.

A growth mindset is the belief that our abilities and intelligence can be developed through dedication, effort, and a willingness to learn. It is the opposite of a fixed mindset, which believes that our qualities are fixed traits and cannot be changed. By recognizing that we have the capacity to grow and improve, we open ourselves up to new possibilities and opportunities.

To cultivate a growth mindset, it is essential to embrace challenges. Instead of shying away from difficult tasks, see them as opportunities for growth and learning. Challenges push us out of our comfort zones, allowing us to develop new skills and expand our knowledge. Remember that setbacks and failures are part of the learning process. Don't let them discourage you, but rather view them as stepping stones towards improvement.

Another key aspect of a growth mindset is the belief in the power of effort and hard work. Understand that mastery and success come through consistent practice and dedication. Effort is not a sign of weakness or incompetence; it is the fuel that drives progress. Embrace a strong work ethic, and you will see your abilities and accomplishments flourish.

In addition to challenges and effort, a growth mindset also values the power of learning. Embrace a lifelong love of learning and continuously seek new knowledge and skills. Be open to feedback and constructive criticism, as they provide opportunities for growth and improvement. Surround yourself with people who inspire and encourage you to reach your full potential.

By cultivating a growth mindset, you will transform your habits and mindset, ultimately leading to greater self-discipline. You will be more resilient in the face of obstacles, more motivated to overcome challenges, and more willing to put in the necessary effort to achieve your goals. Remember, anyone can develop a growth mindset with dedication and practice. So, start embracing challenges, valuing effort, and fostering a love of learning. Unlock your full potential and transform your life through the power of a growth mindset.

Establishing a Supportive Environment

When it comes to developing self-discipline, one crucial factor that often goes unnoticed is the environment we surround ourselves with. Our surroundings play a significant role in shaping our habits, mindset, and ultimately our level of self-discipline. Whether we realize it or not, our environment has a profound impact on our ability to stay focused, motivated, and committed to our goals.

Creating a supportive environment is essential for anyone looking to cultivate self-discipline in their lives. By consciously designing our surroundings to align with our goals and values, we can significantly enhance our chances of success. Here are a few key strategies to establish a supportive environment that fosters self-discipline.

First and foremost, declutter your physical space. A cluttered and chaotic environment can be a major obstacle to self-discipline. Clutter creates distractions and makes it difficult to stay focused. Start by organizing your workspace, home, and personal belongings. Clear out unnecessary items and create a clean, tidy environment that promotes clarity of thought.

Secondly, surround yourself with positive influences. The people we spend our time with have a tremendous impact on our mindset and behavior. Seek out individuals who share your values and goals, as they will provide support and encouragement along your journey of self-discipline. Engage in conversations and activities that inspire and motivate you towards your desired outcomes.

Additionally, consider the impact of digital distractions on your self-discipline. With the prevalence of smartphones and constant online connectivity, it is crucial to set boundaries and create a digital environment that supports your self-discipline. Limit your screen time, turn off notifications, and create designated periods for focused work or personal development.

Lastly, establish daily routines and rituals that reinforce self-discipline. Designing a structure in your day helps to eliminate decision fatigue and creates a sense of order and consistency. Plan your day in advance, schedule time for activities that align with your goals, and commit to sticking to your plan.

Remember, your environment can either enhance or hinder your self-discipline. By consciously creating a supportive environment that promotes focus, positivity, and consistency, you are setting yourself up for success. Take the time to declutter, surround yourself with positive influences, manage digital distractions, and establish daily routines. With a supportive environment in place, you will find it easier to develop and maintain the self-discipline necessary to transform your habits and mindset.

Chapter 4: Developing Self-Discipline in Daily Life

Prioritizing Tasks and Time Management

In our fast-paced world, it's easy to feel overwhelmed by the ever-increasing demands on our time and attention. However, mastering the art of prioritizing tasks and time management can make all the difference in leading a successful and fulfilling life. This subchapter explores the crucial skills of self-discipline, focusing on how to effectively prioritize tasks and manage your time.

Self-discipline is the cornerstone of personal and professional success. It is the ability to make conscious choices and take deliberate actions that align with our goals and values, even when faced with distractions or obstacles. By cultivating self-discipline, we can create a sense of purpose and direction in our lives, enabling us to make the most of our time and achieve our desired outcomes.

One of the first steps in prioritizing tasks is to identify what truly matters to us. By clarifying our goals and values, we can align our actions with our long-term aspirations. This involves reflecting on our priorities, both short-term and long-term, and making conscious decisions about how we allocate our time and energy.

Effective time management is another key aspect of prioritizing tasks. It involves setting clear goals and breaking them down into manageable chunks. By creating a schedule or to-do list, we can stay focused and ensure that we allocate sufficient time to each task. It's important to be realistic about what can be achieved in a given timeframe and to build in time for breaks and relaxation, as self-care is crucial for maintaining productivity and well-being.

When it comes to prioritizing tasks, it's essential to differentiate between urgent and important activities. Urgent tasks may demand immediate attention, but they may not necessarily contribute to our long-term goals. On the other hand, important tasks align with our values and have a significant impact on our desired outcomes. By focusing on important tasks first, we can avoid getting caught up in a cycle of constantly putting out fires and instead make progress towards our goals.

In this subchapter, we will delve deeper into various strategies and techniques for prioritizing tasks and managing time effectively. From setting SMART goals to utilizing time management tools and strategies, we will explore practical tips that can be applied by anyone seeking to enhance their self-discipline and achieve more in their personal and professional lives.

Remember, mastering the art of prioritizing tasks and managing time is not just about being productive; it's about aligning your actions with your values and creating a life that is meaningful and fulfilling. By developing self-discipline and implementing effective time management strategies, you can take control of your time and transform your habits and mindset, ultimately leading to a more successful and rewarding life.

Overcoming Procrastination and Distractions

Introduction:

In today's fast-paced world, we often find ourselves struggling with procrastination and distractions that hinder our progress and prevent us from reaching our full potential. The ability to overcome these obstacles is crucial for personal growth and success. In this subchapter, we will explore effective strategies to develop self-discipline and combat procrastination and distractions.

Understanding Procrastination:

Procrastination is the act of delaying or postponing tasks, often resulting in stress, missed opportunities, and compromised productivity. It is essential to grasp the underlying causes of procrastination to address it effectively. Fear of failure, lack of motivation, and perfectionism are common culprits. By acknowledging and understanding these factors, we can devise a plan to overcome procrastination.

Developing Self-Discipline:

Self-discipline is the key to overcoming procrastination and distractions. By cultivating this invaluable habit, we can boost our productivity, achieve our goals, and transform our lives. One way to develop self-discipline is to set clear, realistic goals and establish a structured schedule. Breaking down tasks into smaller, manageable parts can also alleviate feelings of overwhelm and increase motivation.

Managing Distractions:

Living in the digital age, distractions are everywhere, making it challenging to stay focused. From social media notifications to constant email alerts, the temptation to veer off course is ever-present. To combat distractions effectively, it is crucial to create an environment conducive to concentration. This may involve turning off notifications, designating specific work areas, or using productivity tools like time management apps or website blockers.

Practical Strategies:

There are several practical strategies that can aid in overcoming procrastination and distractions. One effective technique is the "Pomodoro Technique," which involves working for a set period, such as 25 minutes, followed by a short break. This method helps maintain focus and prevents burnout. Additionally, implementing a reward system can provide motivation and serve as an incentive to finish tasks promptly.

Conclusion:

Overcoming procrastination and distractions is a vital skill to cultivate in today's world. By understanding the causes of procrastination, developing self-discipline, and implementing practical strategies, we can break free from the shackles of procrastination and distractions. By harnessing the power of self-discipline, we can transform our habits and mindset, paving the way for personal growth and success. Remember, it is never too late to start on the path of self-discipline and overcome any obstacles that stand in your way. Take control of your life, embrace self-discipline, and unlock your true potential.

Building Consistency and Persistence

Consistency and persistence are two crucial elements when it comes to achieving success in any aspect of life. Whether it's pursuing personal goals, professional growth, or developing healthy habits, the power of self-discipline is what separates those who achieve their dreams from those who don't. In this subchapter, we will explore the strategies and mindset needed to build consistency and persistence, ultimately transforming your habits and mindset.

Consistency is the key to progress. It is about showing up every day, regardless of the circumstances. When we are consistent, we create a routine that helps us stay focused and motivated. Consistency requires discipline and a strong commitment to the journey, even when things get tough. It means making a conscious decision to prioritize our goals and taking small steps consistently, rather than expecting overnight success.

Persistence, on the other hand, is the ability to bounce back from setbacks and keep pushing forward. It is about maintaining a positive mindset even in the face of challenges and failures. Persistence requires resilience and the belief that failure is not the end, but rather a stepping stone towards success. With persistence, we learn from our mistakes, adapt our strategies, and keep moving forward.

To build consistency and persistence, it is crucial to set clear goals and create a plan of action. Break down your goals into smaller, manageable tasks, and create a timeline to track your progress. By setting achievable milestones, you can celebrate small wins along the way, which will fuel your motivation and help you stay consistent.

Another important aspect is to cultivate self-discipline. Self-discipline is the ability to control your impulses and stay focused on your goals. It requires making conscious choices, even when they are not easy or convenient. By practicing self-discipline, you train your mind to resist distractions and stay committed to your path.

Furthermore, surround yourself with a supportive network. Building consistency and persistence can be challenging, and having people who believe in you and your goals can make a significant difference. Seek out mentors, join accountability groups, or find like-minded individuals who can provide guidance and encouragement.

Remember, building consistency and persistence is a journey, not a destination. It requires patience, perseverance, and a growth mindset. Embrace the process, learn from each experience, and keep moving forward. By developing these qualities, you will transform your habits and mindset, unlocking the power of self-discipline and achieving the success you desire in all areas of your life.

In conclusion, consistency and persistence are the cornerstones of self-discipline. They are the driving forces that enable individuals to overcome obstacles, stay focused, and achieve their goals. By building consistency and persistence, you are setting yourself up for success and unlocking your true potential.

Managing Stress and Self-Motivation

In our fast-paced and demanding world, stress has become an inevitable part of our lives. Whether it is due to work pressures, personal relationships, or financial concerns, stress can take a toll on our physical and mental well-being. However, with the right strategies and a strong sense of self-discipline, we can effectively manage stress and stay motivated even in the face of adversity.

One of the key aspects of managing stress is recognizing its symptoms and understanding its impact on our lives. Stress can manifest itself in various ways, such as irritability, fatigue, headaches, and difficulty concentrating. By identifying these signs early on, we can take proactive measures to address them.

To effectively manage stress, it is essential to develop healthy coping mechanisms. This can include engaging in regular physical exercise, practicing relaxation techniques like meditation or deep breathing exercises, and seeking social support from friends and family. Additionally, maintaining a balanced and nutritious diet, getting enough sleep, and avoiding excessive alcohol or caffeine intake can also contribute to stress reduction.

Self-discipline plays a crucial role in managing stress as it helps us stay focused and motivated during challenging times. By setting clear goals and priorities, we can allocate our time and energy more effectively, reducing feelings of overwhelm and anxiety. Developing a routine and sticking to it can also provide a sense of structure and stability, which can be particularly helpful during stressful periods.

Moreover, self-motivation is essential for maintaining a positive mindset and overcoming obstacles. Cultivating a growth mindset, where challenges are seen as opportunities for learning and growth, can help us stay motivated and resilient in the face of setbacks. Setting realistic and achievable goals, breaking them down into smaller tasks, and celebrating milestones along the way can also boost our motivation and sense of accomplishment.

In conclusion, managing stress and self-motivation are essential skills in today's fast-paced world. By recognizing the signs of stress and implementing healthy coping mechanisms, we can effectively reduce its impact on our lives. Furthermore, by cultivating self-discipline and self-motivation, we can stay focused, resilient, and motivated even in the face of adversity. Remember, managing stress is a lifelong journey, and it requires consistent effort and self-awareness. With the power of self-discipline, we can transform our habits and mindset, leading to a more fulfilling and balanced life.

Chapter 5: Strengthening Self-Discipline in Relationships

Nurturing Healthy Boundaries

In the journey of self-discipline, one of the most crucial aspects is understanding and implementing healthy boundaries. Boundaries are the invisible lines that define what is acceptable and what is not in our interactions, relationships, and behavior. They serve as a protective shield, safeguarding our emotional and mental well-being, and allowing us to maintain a healthy balance in our lives.

Setting and maintaining healthy boundaries is an essential skill that everyone can benefit from. Whether you are a student, a professional, a parent, or simply someone striving for personal growth, nurturing healthy boundaries will empower you to lead a more fulfilling and disciplined life.

First and foremost, it is important to recognize your own needs and values. Take the time to reflect on what is truly important to you and what you need in order to thrive. By understanding your own limits and desires, you can effectively communicate them to others, fostering healthier and more respectful relationships.

Boundaries are not meant to be rigid walls; rather, they should be flexible and adaptable. It is crucial to learn how to say no when necessary and assertively express your limits and boundaries. This will help you avoid being overwhelmed or taken advantage of, allowing you to allocate your time and energy effectively.

Additionally, nurturing healthy boundaries requires self-awareness and self-care. It is important to prioritize your own well-being and make time for activities that replenish your energy and bring you joy. By taking care of yourself, you are better equipped to show up fully in your relationships and commitments.

In the pursuit of self-discipline, it is also vital to recognize when boundaries are being crossed or violated. If someone consistently disrespects your boundaries, it may be necessary to reevaluate the relationship or seek support from a trusted friend or professional. Remember, setting boundaries is not selfish; it is an act of self-respect and self-preservation.

Lastly, nurturing healthy boundaries involves practicing empathy and respect for others' boundaries as well. By acknowledging and honoring the boundaries of those around you, you create an environment of mutual respect and understanding.

In conclusion, nurturing healthy boundaries is a crucial component of self-discipline. It empowers us to lead balanced and fulfilling lives, prioritize our well-being, and cultivate respectful relationships. By understanding our own needs and values, communicating assertively, practicing self-care, and respecting the boundaries of others, we can create a harmonious and disciplined existence. Embrace the power of healthy boundaries, and watch as your self-discipline and overall happiness soar to new heights.

Communicating Effectively and Assertively

In our daily lives, effective communication plays a vital role in building relationships, resolving conflicts, and achieving our goals. Whether it's expressing our needs and desires, giving feedback, or setting boundaries, the way we communicate can greatly impact the outcomes we desire. In the realm of self-discipline, mastering the art of effective and assertive communication is crucial for personal growth and success.

Effective communication involves expressing ourselves clearly and being understood by others. It requires active listening, empathy, and a willingness to understand different perspectives. By communicating effectively, we can avoid misunderstandings, build trust, and foster positive connections with others. In the context of self-discipline, this skill is essential for setting boundaries and maintaining healthy habits.

Assertive communication, on the other hand, involves expressing our thoughts, feelings, and needs in a direct and respectful manner. It enables us to stand up for ourselves, assert our rights, and negotiate effectively. Being assertive allows us to communicate our desires and expectations without being aggressive or passive. In the context of self-discipline, assertive communication empowers us to say no to distractions, set clear goals, and prioritize our time and energy effectively.

To communicate effectively and assertively, it's important to cultivate self-awareness. Understanding our own emotions, needs, and values will enable us to communicate authentically. Additionally, practicing active listening and empathy will help us better understand others' perspectives, fostering stronger relationships and collaboration.

Furthermore, effective and assertive communication can be enhanced by using clear and concise language, maintaining good eye contact, and employing confident body language. By practicing these techniques, we can convey our messages with clarity and conviction, increasing the chances of being heard and understood.

In the journey of self-discipline, effective and assertive communication is a powerful tool that can help us overcome challenges, resist temptations, and stay focused on our goals. By mastering this skill, we can effectively communicate our needs and desires, navigate conflicts, and build supportive networks that foster our personal growth and success.

Remember, communication is not just about speaking; it's about listening, understanding, and connecting with others. By honing our communication skills, we can transform our habits and mindset, unlocking the true power of self-discipline in our lives.

Resisting Peer Pressure and Temptation

In today's fast-paced and increasingly connected world, it has become even more challenging to resist the constant pressures and temptations that surround us. Whether it's the influence of our peers or the lure of instant gratification, maintaining self-discipline is crucial for achieving personal growth and success. In this subchapter, we will explore effective strategies to resist peer pressure and temptation, empowering you to take control of your life and make choices aligned with your values and long-term goals.

It's important to understand that peer pressure and temptation are natural aspects of human interaction. We all desire acceptance and validation from our peers, making it harder to go against the crowd. However, true strength lies in staying true to yourself and your principles, even when faced with external pressures. By cultivating self-awareness and understanding your values, you will be better equipped to resist negative influences.

One powerful technique to resist peer pressure is to surround yourself with like-minded individuals who share your values and goals. By building a strong support network, you can find encouragement and inspiration to stay on track. Additionally, it's essential to develop assertiveness skills, enabling you to confidently express your opinions and say "no" when faced with temptations that conflict with your values.

Another crucial aspect of resisting peer pressure and temptation is developing a strong sense of self-discipline. Self-discipline is the ability to control your impulses and make choices that serve your long-term goals. It requires commitment, consistency, and a deep understanding of delayed gratification. By practicing self-discipline regularly, you strengthen your willpower and become more resilient to external pressures.

Moreover, setting clear goals and creating a roadmap for yourself can greatly help in resisting temptations. When you have a clear vision of where you want to be, it becomes easier to make choices that align with your aspirations. Remember to break down your goals into smaller, manageable steps, and celebrate each milestone along the way. This will keep you motivated and focused on your journey.

In conclusion, resisting peer pressure and temptation is a fundamental aspect of self-discipline. By cultivating self-awareness, surrounding yourself with supportive individuals, developing assertiveness skills, practicing self-discipline, and setting clear goals, you can overcome external influences and stay true to your values. Remember, the power to resist lies within you – embrace it and unleash the full potential of self-discipline in transforming your habits and mindset.

Fostering Accountability and Support Systems

Self-discipline is a powerful tool that can transform your habits and mindset, enabling you to achieve your goals and live a fulfilling life. However, maintaining self-discipline can be challenging, especially when faced with temptations, distractions, and setbacks. That's where fostering accountability and support systems come into play.

Accountability is the key to staying on track with your self-discipline journey. By holding yourself accountable, you take responsibility for your actions and their consequences. It involves setting clear goals, creating a plan, and regularly monitoring your progress. However, it can be difficult to maintain accountability solely on your own.

That's where support systems become essential. Surrounding yourself with like-minded individuals who share your desire for self-discipline can provide the necessary support and encouragement to stay focused. Whether it's a mentor, a coach, or a group of friends, having someone to hold you accountable can make a significant difference in your self-discipline journey.

One effective way to foster accountability is by creating an accountability partner or joining an accountability group. These individuals or communities not only provide support but also help you stay committed to your goals. Regular check-ins, sharing progress, and discussing challenges can help you stay motivated and overcome obstacles.

Additionally, support systems can offer valuable insights, guidance, and advice. They can share their own experiences and strategies for maintaining self-discipline, providing you with invaluable resources to enhance your own journey. Moreover, being part of a community where everyone is pursuing self-discipline can create a sense of camaraderie and inspiration.

To foster accountability and support systems, it's important to be open and vulnerable. Share your goals and challenges with your accountability partner or group, and be willing to receive constructive feedback. This openness allows you to learn from others' experiences and grow as you work towards your self-discipline goals.

Remember, self-discipline is a lifelong journey, and having a strong support system is crucial to maintaining it. By fostering accountability and surrounding yourself with individuals who share your passion for self-discipline, you can overcome obstacles, stay motivated, and achieve remarkable personal growth.

In conclusion, fostering accountability and support systems is a vital aspect of developing and maintaining self-discipline. By creating an accountability partner or joining an accountability group, you can enhance your commitment and motivation towards your goals. Embracing the support and guidance from others will help you navigate challenges and achieve long-term success in your self-discipline journey.

Accountability and support systems are essential components in the journey of self-discipline. They provide the necessary structure and guidance to help individuals stay on track and achieve their goals. Whether you are striving to improve your health, advance in your career, or develop new habits, having a robust support system and holding yourself accountable can make a world of difference.

One of the key aspects of fostering accountability is setting clear and specific goals. Without a target to aim for, it becomes challenging to measure progress and stay motivated. By defining your objectives in a precise manner, you create a roadmap that outlines the steps needed to reach them. This clarity allows you to track your progress and make adjustments along the way.

In addition to setting goals, it is crucial to establish a system of checks and balances. This can be done through self-monitoring or by involving someone else who can help hold you accountable. For example, if you are trying to establish a regular exercise routine, you can track your workouts and progress in a journal or use a fitness app to monitor your activity. Alternatively, you can enlist the help of a workout buddy who shares similar goals and can provide support and motivation.

Creating a support system is equally important in maintaining self-discipline. Surrounding yourself with individuals who share your values and aspirations can significantly impact your success. These individuals can offer encouragement, provide constructive feedback, and hold you accountable when needed. Building relationships with like-minded people through networking events, online communities, or joining relevant clubs and organizations can help foster a strong support system.

In addition to personal connections, utilizing technological tools can also be beneficial in fostering accountability and support. There are numerous apps and online platforms available that can assist in tracking habits, managing goals, and connecting with others on a similar journey. These resources provide a virtual support system that can be accessed anytime, anywhere.

Ultimately, fostering accountability and support systems is about creating an environment that promotes self-discipline and encourages growth. By setting clear goals, establishing checks and balances, and surrounding yourself with a supportive network, you can overcome obstacles and achieve your desired outcomes. Remember, self-discipline is a journey, and having a strong support system and accountability measures in place will help you stay on the path to success.

In our journey towards self-discipline, one of the crucial aspects that often gets overlooked is the need for accountability and support systems. While it may seem daunting to some, creating a solid foundation of accountability and support can significantly enhance our ability to transform our habits and mindset.

Accountability acts as a powerful tool to keep us on track and motivated. When we have someone to answer to or share our progress with, we are more likely to stay committed to our goals. Consider finding an accountability partner - someone who shares similar aspirations and is also striving for self-discipline. This can be a friend, a family member, or even a colleague. By regularly checking in with each other, sharing successes, and holding each other accountable, you can create a supportive environment that fuels your discipline.

Another effective way to foster accountability is through public commitment. Share your goals with others, whether it's through social media or a personal blog. By making your intentions public, you are more likely to follow through and avoid the embarrassment of not living up to your own words.

In addition to accountability, building a strong support system is equally crucial. Surround yourself with individuals who uplift and encourage you on your journey towards self-discipline. Seek out like-minded individuals who share your passion for personal growth and self-improvement. Attend workshops, seminars, or join online communities that focus on self-discipline. By connecting with others who are on a similar path, you will find the inspiration and motivation needed to push through challenges.

Moreover, it is vital to remember that self-discipline is not a solitary pursuit. It is essential to lean on others during times of struggle or setbacks. Reach out to your support system when you need guidance, advice, or simply a listening ear. Sharing your challenges and seeking help does not indicate weakness; it demonstrates your commitment to personal growth.

Remember, fostering accountability and support systems is not a sign of dependency, but rather an acknowledgment of the power of collective strength. By surrounding yourself with individuals who hold you accountable and provide support, you are setting yourself up for success on your journey towards self-discipline. Embrace these systems, and watch as they transform your habits and mindset, enabling you to unlock your true potential.

Chapter 6: Overcoming Obstacles and Challenges

Dealing with Failure and Setbacks

Failure and setbacks are inevitable parts of life. No matter how disciplined we are, there will always be times when things don't go as planned. However, it's how we deal with these failures and setbacks that truly define our character and determine our success. In this subchapter, we will explore effective strategies for overcoming these obstacles and turning them into opportunities for growth.

One of the first things to remember is that failure is not the end of the road. It's merely a detour on the path to success. Instead of dwelling on your mistakes and beating yourself up, shift your mindset to view failure as a valuable learning experience. Ask yourself: What can I learn from this setback? How can I use it to improve myself and my approach? By reframing failure in this way, you can bounce back stronger and more determined than ever before.

Another key aspect of dealing with failure is resilience. Developing a resilient mindset allows you to navigate through setbacks without losing sight of your goals. Cultivate the belief that setbacks are temporary and that you have the ability to overcome any challenge. Embrace the power of perseverance and refuse to let failure define you. Remember, success is not achieved overnight; it's a result of consistent effort and determination.

Additionally, it's important to surround yourself with a support system that encourages and uplifts you during difficult times. Seek out mentors, friends, or family members who can provide guidance and perspective. By sharing your struggles with others, you not only gain valuable insights but also realize that you are not alone in facing setbacks. Together, you can find solace, motivation, and encouragement to keep going.

Lastly, self-compassion plays a crucial role in dealing with failure and setbacks. Treat yourself with kindness and understanding, just as you would a close friend. Acknowledge your emotions and allow yourself to grieve or feel disappointed. However, also remind yourself that setbacks are not a reflection of your worth or abilities. Practice self-care and self-compassion to rebuild your confidence and strengthen your resilience.

In conclusion, failure and setbacks are an unavoidable part of life, but they don't have to define us. By adopting a growth mindset, cultivating resilience, seeking support, and practicing self-compassion, we can turn failures into stepping stones towards success. Remember, setbacks are not permanent roadblocks; they are opportunities for growth and self-improvement. Embrace them, learn from them, and let them fuel your journey towards becoming the best version of yourself.

Failure and setbacks are an inevitable part of life, and they can often be disheartening and demotivating. However, it is crucial to understand that these challenges are not roadblocks but opportunities for growth and learning. In the realm of self-discipline, it is essential to develop strategies to effectively deal with failure and setbacks, as they are bound to occur on the path to success.

One of the first steps in handling failure and setbacks is to shift your mindset. Instead of viewing them as personal shortcomings or signs of incompetence, see them as valuable learning experiences. Embrace failure as a stepping stone towards progress and improvement. Remember, every successful person has encountered numerous setbacks along the way.

It is also important to analyze the reasons behind the failure or setback. Take a step back and objectively evaluate the situation. Identify any mistakes or missteps that may have led to the outcome. By understanding the root causes, you can make necessary adjustments and avoid repeating the same mistakes in the future.

Another crucial aspect of dealing with failure is to maintain a positive attitude. It is easy to get discouraged and lose motivation when things don't go as planned. However, it is vital to remain optimistic and resilient. Cultivate a positive mindset that enables you to see setbacks as temporary obstacles that can be overcome with determination and perseverance.

In addition, seek support from others during challenging times. Surround yourself with individuals who believe in your abilities and can offer constructive advice and encouragement. Share your experiences and setbacks with trusted friends, family, or mentors who can provide valuable insights and guidance.

Furthermore, practicing self-compassion is essential when facing failure and setbacks. Treat yourself with kindness and understanding, just as you would a close friend. Understand that setbacks are a natural part of the journey towards success and that everyone makes mistakes.

Learn from the experience, forgive yourself, and use it as motivation to continue pushing forward.

Finally, it is crucial to maintain a long-term perspective. Remember that setbacks are temporary and do not define your overall journey. Stay focused on your goals, and don't allow failure to derail your progress. Develop resilience and keep moving forward, knowing that success is ultimately achieved through perseverance and self-discipline.

In conclusion, failure and setbacks are inevitable in the pursuit of self-discipline. By shifting your mindset, analyzing the reasons behind the setback, maintaining a positive attitude, seeking support, practicing self-compassion, and maintaining a long-term perspective, you can effectively deal with and overcome any setback on your path towards personal growth and success. Embrace failure as an opportunity for learning, and let it fuel your determination to become the best version of yourself.

Failure and setbacks are an inevitable part of life. We all face challenges and stumble on our journey towards success. However, it is not the failures that define us, but how we respond to them. In the realm of self-discipline, learning how to deal with failure and setbacks is crucial for personal growth and transformation.

First and foremost, it is important to reframe the way we perceive failure. Rather than viewing it as a negative outcome, we should see it as an opportunity for learning and growth. Each failure provides valuable lessons that can help us improve and become better versions of ourselves. By changing our mindset, we can transform failure into a stepping stone towards success.

In the face of failure, it is easy to become disheartened and lose motivation. However, this is precisely the time when self-discipline becomes most crucial. It is during these challenging moments that we need to dig deep and find the determination to keep pushing forward. Self-discipline allows us to stay focused on our goals, even in the face of adversity.

When setbacks occur, it is important to reflect on what went wrong and identify the areas that need improvement. By taking a proactive approach and analyzing our failures, we can identify patterns and make necessary adjustments. Self-discipline plays a crucial role in this process, as it requires us to take responsibility for our actions and make the necessary changes to move forward.

Furthermore, it is important to surround ourselves with a supportive network of individuals who understand the value of self-discipline. Having a strong support system can help us navigate through failures and setbacks more effectively. These individuals can provide guidance, encouragement, and accountability, ensuring that we stay on the path of self-discipline even in the face of adversity.

In conclusion, failure and setbacks are an integral part of the journey towards success. Learning how to deal with them effectively is essential for personal growth and transformation. By reframing our mindset, staying disciplined, reflecting on our failures, and seeking support from others, we can overcome any setback and continue on the path of self-discipline. Remember, it is not the failures that define us, but how we respond to them that truly matters.

Handling Impulsivity and Instant Gratification

In today's fast-paced world, where everything is just a click away, it has become increasingly challenging to resist the allure of instant gratification. Whether it's indulging in unhealthy food, impulsive shopping, or mindlessly scrolling through social media, we often find ourselves succumbing to our impulsive desires. However, by cultivating self-discipline, we can regain control over our actions and make conscious choices that align with our long-term goals and values.

Understanding the root causes of impulsivity is the first step towards overcoming it. Impulsivity often arises from a need to escape discomfort or fill an emotional void. We seek temporary relief in the form of immediate pleasure, but this only perpetuates a cycle of short-term satisfaction and long-term dissatisfaction. Recognizing this pattern allows us to break free from it and make intentional decisions that prioritize our well-being.

Developing self-discipline requires a combination of mindset shifts and practical strategies. One effective approach is to identify and redefine our goals, both short-term and long-term. By clarifying what truly matters to us, we can align our actions accordingly. This process involves evaluating the potential consequences of our impulsive choices and weighing them against our desired outcomes. Are the fleeting moments of gratification worth sacrificing our long-term success and happiness?

Another useful technique is to create a buffer between our impulses and actions. This can be achieved by implementing a "pause and reflect" strategy. Whenever we feel the urge to give in to instant gratification, we consciously pause, take a deep breath, and reflect on our intentions. This momentary pause allows us to regain control over our impulses and make a more deliberate decision. Over time, this practice strengthens our self-discipline muscle, making it easier to resist impulsive temptations.

Furthermore, cultivating mindfulness can greatly support our efforts to handle impulsivity. By practicing present-moment awareness, we become more attuned to our thoughts, emotions, and physical sensations. This heightened self-awareness helps us identify the triggers that lead to impulsive behavior and enables us to respond rather than react. Mindfulness also allows us to appreciate the beauty of delayed gratification, as we become more receptive to the long-term benefits that come from resisting instant pleasures.

In conclusion, handling impulsivity and instant gratification is a fundamental aspect of self-discipline. By recognizing the underlying causes of impulsivity, redefining our goals, creating buffers, and practicing mindfulness, we can break free from the cycle of instant gratification and make choices that serve our long-term well-being. It is through self-discipline that we can transform our habits and mindset, ultimately leading to a more fulfilling and purposeful life.

In today's fast-paced world, where everything is just a click away, we often find ourselves falling victim to impulsivity and the allure of instant gratification. The constant bombardment of advertisements and social media feeds leaves us craving for more, making it increasingly difficult to practice self-discipline. However, learning to handle impulsivity and instant gratification is crucial if we want to transform our habits and mindset.

Impulsivity is the tendency to act without thinking, giving in to our immediate desires or temptations. It can lead to poor decision-making, regret, and a lack of control over our lives. Instant gratification, on the other hand, refers to the desire for immediate pleasure or satisfaction, often at the expense of long-term goals or well-being.

To combat impulsivity and instant gratification, we must first understand the reasons behind our impulsive behavior. It could be a coping mechanism for stress, boredom, or a desire to escape reality. By identifying these triggers, we can develop alternative strategies to address our underlying needs without resorting to impulsive actions.

One effective technique is to create a pause between our impulses and actions. Instead of immediately giving in to our desires, we can take a deep breath, count to ten, or engage in a different activity to distract ourselves. This pause allows us to evaluate the consequences of our actions and make a more rational decision, aligning with our long-term goals.

Another powerful tool is to practice delayed gratification. This involves consciously delaying the fulfillment of our immediate desires in favor of achieving more significant rewards in the future. By setting specific goals and breaking them down into smaller milestones, we can maintain focus and motivation, even when faced with short-term temptations.

Building self-discipline is a gradual process that requires consistent effort and practice. It involves setting clear boundaries, establishing routines, and developing a growth mindset. Surrounding ourselves with like-minded individuals who value self-discipline can also provide the necessary support and accountability.

Ultimately, handling impulsivity and instant gratification requires a shift in mindset. It is about recognizing that true fulfillment and success come from delayed gratification and making choices aligned with our long-term goals. By mastering self-discipline, we gain control over our impulses and pave the way for a more fulfilling and purpose-driven life. So, let us embark on this journey of self-discovery and transform our habits and mindset to unleash the power of self-discipline within us.

Impulsivity and instant gratification can be major obstacles on the path to self-discipline. In today's fast-paced and convenience-driven world, it is easy to give in to our desires and make impulsive decisions that may not align with our long-term goals. However, learning how to handle impulsivity and resist instant gratification is crucial for personal growth and success. In this subchapter, we will explore effective strategies to help you overcome these challenges and develop a stronger sense of self-discipline.

One of the first steps in handling impulsivity is understanding the root causes behind it. Impulsive behavior often stems from a lack of self-awareness and emotional regulation. By becoming more mindful of our thoughts, feelings, and triggers, we can better understand why we engage in impulsive actions. This self-awareness will allow us to take a step back and assess the consequences of our actions before acting on them.

Another key aspect of handling impulsivity is developing a plan of action. Setting clear goals and creating a roadmap towards achieving them can help us stay focused and avoid impulsive detours. Breaking down our goals into smaller, manageable tasks provides a sense of accomplishment and progress, reducing the urge for instant gratification.

Furthermore, practicing delayed gratification is essential for strengthening self-discipline. Instant gratification often leads to short-term pleasure but long-term regret. By learning to delay gratification, we can build resilience and develop the ability to resist temptations that hinder our progress. This could involve setting aside time for reflection before making impulsive decisions or finding healthier alternatives to satisfy our immediate cravings.

Building a support system is also crucial in handling impulsivity and instant gratification. Surrounding ourselves with like-minded individuals who share our commitment to self-discipline can help us stay motivated and accountable. Engaging in activities that promote self-discipline, such as joining a gym or participating in group challenges, can provide additional support and reinforcement.

Ultimately, handling impulsivity and instant gratification is a continuous journey that requires practice and patience. By implementing these strategies and adopting a growth mindset, we can gradually overcome these obstacles and transform our habits and mindset. With self-discipline as our guide, we can achieve our long-term goals and lead a more fulfilling and successful life.

Remember, self-discipline is not about denying ourselves pleasure but rather about making conscious choices that align with our values and long-term aspirations. Embracing delayed gratification and resisting impulsive urges can lead to greater self-control, improved decision-making, and a sense of empowerment. So, let us embark on this journey together and unlock the power of self-discipline within ourselves.

Overcoming Procrastination and Laziness

In today's fast-paced world, where distractions are abundant and demands on our time and attention never seem to cease, it can be challenging to maintain self-discipline and avoid falling into the traps of procrastination and laziness. However, with the right mindset and strategies, it is possible to overcome these obstacles and unlock the power of self-discipline.

Procrastination and laziness are common issues that affect people from all walks of life. Whether you are a student, an entrepreneur, or a professional, these habits can hinder your progress and prevent you from reaching your full potential. Fortunately, there are proven techniques that can help you break free from the grip of procrastination and laziness.

The first step towards overcoming procrastination and laziness is to understand their root causes. Often, these habits stem from fear, lack of motivation, or a sense of overwhelm. By identifying and addressing these underlying factors, you can begin to take control of your actions and develop a more disciplined mindset.

One effective strategy is to break tasks into smaller, manageable chunks. When faced with a daunting project or a mountain of work, it is easy to become overwhelmed and succumb to the temptation of procrastination. However, by breaking tasks down into smaller, more achievable steps, you can make progress and build momentum, which will help to combat procrastination and keep you motivated.

Another powerful technique is to create a schedule or a to-do list. By mapping out your day and prioritizing tasks, you can stay organized and focused. This not only helps to prevent procrastination but also allows you to allocate time for relaxation and self-care, which are crucial for maintaining a healthy work-life balance.

Furthermore, it is essential to cultivate self-awareness and mindfulness. Pay attention to your thoughts and emotions, and be honest with yourself about any tendencies towards procrastination or laziness. By staying present and aware, you can catch yourself in the act and redirect your focus towards more productive activities.

Finally, surround yourself with a supportive environment. Seek out like-minded individuals who are also striving for self-discipline and avoiding procrastination. Share your goals and challenges with them, and hold each other accountable. Additionally, limit exposure to distractions such as social media or television, and create a conducive workspace that promotes focus and productivity.

In conclusion, overcoming procrastination and laziness is a journey that requires self-awareness, discipline, and perseverance. By understanding the underlying causes, implementing effective strategies, and cultivating a supportive environment, you can break free from these habits and unlock your full potential. Remember, the power of self-discipline lies within you, and with determination and commitment, you can transform your habits and mindset to achieve success in all areas of your life.

Procrastination and laziness are two common obstacles that hinder personal growth and success. We all experience moments of weakness when we lack motivation or find ourselves putting off important tasks.

However, with the power of self-discipline, we can overcome these tendencies and transform our habits and mindset for the better.

Procrastination is the act of delaying or postponing tasks, often opting for instant gratification or short-term pleasure instead. It is a habit that can have detrimental effects on our productivity, efficiency, and ultimately, our overall success. Similarly, laziness is the habit of avoiding effort or exertion, choosing comfort over progress. Both of these tendencies can leave us feeling unfulfilled and stuck in a cycle of mediocrity.

To overcome procrastination and laziness, self-discipline is key. It is the ability to control our impulses, stay focused on our goals, and take consistent action towards achieving them. It requires a shift in mindset and the development of new habits that support our long-term aspirations.

One effective strategy to combat procrastination and laziness is to break tasks into smaller, manageable steps. By doing so, we can make the task at hand feel less overwhelming and more achievable. Set specific deadlines for each step and hold yourself accountable to meet them. This approach not only enhances productivity but also provides a sense of accomplishment as you progress through each milestone.

Another powerful technique is to eliminate distractions. Identify the factors that often derail your focus and take proactive steps to minimize their influence. This may involve turning off notifications on your phone, creating a dedicated workspace, or establishing a routine that promotes concentration and productivity. By creating an environment conducive to work, you can minimize the temptation to procrastinate or succumb to laziness.

Additionally, cultivating a strong sense of purpose and envisioning your desired outcome can be highly motivating. Understand why the task at hand is important to you and how it aligns with your long-term goals. Visualize the satisfaction and fulfillment that will come from completing it. This mindset shift will fuel your determination and help you push through moments of laziness or the temptation to procrastinate.

Remember, overcoming procrastination and laziness is a continuous process. It requires consistent effort and self-awareness. However, by practicing self-discipline and adopting these strategies, you can break free from the grip of procrastination and laziness, unlocking your full potential and transforming your habits and mindset for a more successful and fulfilling life.

Introduction

Procrastination and laziness are common obstacles that hinder personal growth and success. In this subchapter, we will explore powerful strategies to overcome these challenges and develop self-discipline. By cultivating self-discipline, you will be able to transform your habits and mindset, leading to a more fulfilling and productive life.

Understanding Procrastination and Laziness

Procrastination often stems from fear, perfectionism, or a lack of motivation. It is the act of delaying or avoiding tasks that need to be accomplished. Laziness, on the other hand, is a state of unwillingness to exert effort or engage in activities that require energy. Both procrastination and laziness can have detrimental effects on our personal and professional lives.

The Power of Self-Discipline

Self-discipline is the key to overcoming procrastination and laziness. It is the ability to control and direct our actions towards achieving our goals, even when faced with distractions or challenges. By developing self-discipline, we can become more focused, motivated, and productive individuals.

Strategies for Overcoming Procrastination

1. Set Clear Goals: Clearly define what you want to achieve and break it down into manageable steps. This will provide you with a sense of direction and purpose.

2. Prioritize Tasks: Identify the most important tasks and tackle them first. This will help prevent you from getting overwhelmed and allow you to make progress towards your goals.

3. Create a Schedule: Develop a daily or weekly schedule that includes specific time slots for different tasks. Stick to this schedule as much as possible, as it will help you stay on track and avoid distractions.

4. Practice Time Management: Learn to manage your time effectively by utilizing techniques such as the Pomodoro Technique, which involves working in short bursts of focused activity followed by short breaks.

Strategies for Overcoming Laziness

1. Find Your Motivation: Identify what truly inspires and motivates you. Whether it's a personal goal, a passion, or a vision for your future, connecting with your motivation will help you overcome laziness.

2. Cultivate Positive Habits: Incorporate healthy habits into your daily routine, such as regular exercise, proper nutrition, and sufficient sleep. These habits will increase your energy levels and combat laziness.

3. Surround Yourself with Supportive People: Surround yourself with individuals who have a strong work ethic and share your desire for self-improvement. Their positive influence will help you stay motivated and accountable.

4. Embrace Accountability: Set deadlines for yourself and share your goals with someone you trust. This will create a sense of accountability and increase your commitment to completing tasks.

Conclusion

Overcoming procrastination and laziness requires a conscious effort to develop self-discipline. By implementing the strategies mentioned in this subchapter, you can transform your habits and mindset, ultimately leading to greater success and personal fulfillment. Remember, self-discipline is a skill that can be cultivated with practice and determination. Start today and unlock the power of self-discipline in your life.

Managing Emotional Triggers and Self-Control

In our journey towards self-discipline, one of the biggest obstacles we face is our emotional triggers. These triggers can derail our progress, causing us to lose control and succumb to our impulses. However, by learning to manage these triggers and strengthening our self-control, we can regain control of our actions and transform our habits and mindset.

Emotional triggers are the catalysts that ignite our instinctive and impulsive responses. They can be anything from a negative comment to a stressful situation. When we encounter these triggers, our emotions can quickly take over, leading us to react in ways that are counterproductive to our goals and aspirations. Managing these triggers is crucial for developing self-discipline.

The first step in managing emotional triggers is becoming aware of them. Take some time to reflect on the situations, people, or events that tend to set you off. By recognizing these triggers, you can start anticipating them and proactively prepare yourself for the emotional response they may evoke.

Once you have identified your triggers, it's essential to develop strategies to maintain self-control in the face of emotional turmoil. One effective technique is practicing mindfulness. By staying present in the moment and observing your thoughts and emotions without judgment, you can create a gap between your triggers and your reactions. This gap allows you to choose a more constructive response rather than being driven solely by your emotions.

Another useful strategy is to build emotional resilience through self-care. Taking care of your physical and mental well-being can help you better manage stressful situations and emotional triggers. Engaging in activities such as exercise, meditation, or spending time with loved ones can help you develop the emotional strength necessary to remain in control when faced with challenging circumstances.

Furthermore, reframing your perspective can also be helpful in managing emotional triggers. Instead of viewing these triggers as threats or problems, try to see them as opportunities for growth and self-improvement. By shifting your mindset, you can approach these triggers with a sense of curiosity and openness, allowing you to learn from them rather than being overwhelmed by them.

Managing emotional triggers and strengthening self-control is an ongoing process that requires patience and persistence. However, by implementing these strategies and committing to your self-discipline journey, you can transform your habits and mindset, ultimately leading to a more fulfilled and successful life.

Remember, self-discipline is not about suppressing your emotions but rather understanding and harnessing them to make conscious choices. By mastering your emotional triggers and cultivating self-control, you can unlock your true potential and create lasting positive change in every aspect of your life.

In our quest for personal growth and success, one of the greatest challenges we face is managing our emotional triggers and exercising self-control. The ability to effectively manage our emotions and impulses can determine whether we achieve our goals or succumb to temporary gratification. In this subchapter, we will explore practical strategies and techniques that can empower every individual to develop self-discipline and master their emotional triggers.

Emotional triggers are those situations or stimuli that elicit strong emotional reactions within us. They can range from encountering stressful circumstances to facing moments of temptation. Understanding our triggers is the first step towards managing them. By identifying patterns and recognizing specific triggers, we can prepare ourselves mentally and emotionally to respond in a more controlled manner.

Self-control is the foundation of self-discipline. It is the ability to resist immediate impulses and instead choose actions that align with our long-term goals. Developing self-control requires practice and perseverance. One effective strategy is to create a pause between the trigger and response. This pause allows us to consider the consequences of our actions, evaluate alternatives, and make a conscious decision rather than acting on impulse.

Another powerful tool in managing emotional triggers is emotional intelligence. By enhancing our emotional intelligence, we can better understand and regulate our emotions. This involves cultivating self-awareness, recognizing our emotional states, and learning to control them effectively. By practicing self-reflection and mindfulness, we can develop the capacity to respond to triggers in a more composed and rational manner.

Furthermore, building a support system is essential in our journey towards self-discipline. Surrounding ourselves with like-minded individuals who share our goals can provide invaluable guidance and encouragement. Sharing our struggles and triumphs with others fosters accountability and reinforces our commitment to self-control.

Lastly, it is important to celebrate small victories along the way. Self-discipline is a lifelong journey, and recognizing and rewarding ourselves for progress made fuels our motivation to continue on the path of self-improvement.

In conclusion, managing emotional triggers and cultivating self-control are vital skills in the pursuit of self-discipline. By understanding our triggers, developing self-control, enhancing emotional intelligence, and building a support system, we can navigate the challenges that come our way. Remember, self-discipline is not about perfection but rather progress. With dedication and perseverance, we can transform our habits and mindset, unlocking the power of self-discipline to achieve our fullest potential.

In our journey to develop self-discipline, one of the most crucial aspects we must address is managing emotional triggers and practicing self-control. Emotions have a powerful influence on our behavior and can often lead us astray from our goals. However, by understanding and effectively managing these triggers, we can regain control over our actions and make significant progress towards our desired outcomes.

Emotional triggers can come in various forms, such as stress, anger, frustration, or even boredom. They have the potential to derail our self-discipline, causing us to engage in impulsive or destructive behaviors. Recognizing these triggers is the first step towards gaining mastery over them. By becoming more self-aware, we can identify the specific situations, people, or thoughts that tend to trigger our emotional responses.

Once we have identified our emotional triggers, the next step is to develop strategies to manage them effectively. One technique is to practice mindfulness, which involves being fully present in the moment and observing our thoughts and emotions without judgment. Mindfulness helps us detach ourselves from intense emotional reactions, allowing us to respond in a more controlled and rational manner.

Another valuable strategy is to create a plan of action for when emotional triggers arise. For instance, if stress tends to lead us to indulge in unhealthy eating habits, we can proactively prepare nutritious snacks or engage in a stress-relieving activity like exercise or meditation. By having a predetermined plan, we reduce the likelihood of succumbing to impulsive behaviors.

In addition to managing emotional triggers, cultivating self-control is fundamental to achieving self-discipline. Self-control is the ability to resist immediate gratification in favor of long-term goals. It requires discipline and practice to overcome the urge for instant gratification and make choices that align with our values and objectives.

To enhance self-control, it is essential to set clear, realistic goals and establish a system of rewards and consequences. Breaking down larger goals into smaller, manageable tasks allows for a sense of accomplishment and motivation along the way. Implementing a rewards system that aligns with our values can serve as a powerful incentive to maintain self-control.

Moreover, surrounding ourselves with a supportive environment can significantly impact our self-control. By associating with individuals who share similar goals and values, we can draw strength and inspiration from their actions and attitudes. On the other hand, minimizing exposure to situations or people that trigger our impulsive tendencies can help safeguard our self-control.

In conclusion, managing emotional triggers and practicing self-control are vital components of self-discipline. By recognizing and understanding our emotional triggers, developing effective strategies to manage them, and cultivating self-control, we can regain control over our actions and transform our habits and mindset. With perseverance and dedication, we can harness the power of self-discipline to achieve our goals and lead a more fulfilling life.

Chapter 7: Sustaining Self-Discipline for Long-Term Success

Celebrating Milestones and Rewards

Subchapter: Celebrating Milestones and Rewards

Introduction:

In our journey of self-discipline, it is crucial to acknowledge and celebrate our milestones and rewards. These moments of recognition not only provide a well-deserved break from our daily routine but also serve as powerful motivators to keep going. By celebrating our achievements, we reinforce positive habits and cultivate a mindset of success. In this subchapter, we will explore the importance of celebrating milestones and rewards in our pursuit of self-discipline and how it can contribute to transforming our habits and mindset.

1.   The   Power   of   Milestones: Milestones mark significant progress on our path of self-discipline. They serve as signposts along the way, reminding us of how far we have come and inspiring us to keep moving forward. Recognizing and celebrating milestones helps us maintain momentum, bolstering our confidence and reinforcing the belief that we can achieve our goals. By breaking our journey into smaller, achievable milestones, we can track our progress and stay motivated throughout the process.

2.   Rewards   as   Motivators: Rewards play a vital role in our journey towards self-discipline. They act as incentives, fueling our determination and commitment. By setting up rewards for ourselves at various milestones, we create a

positive association with our efforts and make the journey more enjoyable. Rewards can be both intrinsic, such as self-praise or personal time, and extrinsic, such as a small treat or outing. They serve as a reminder that our hard work deserves recognition and celebration.

3.   Creating   Effective   Reward   Systems:
To maximize the impact of rewards, it is important to create effective reward systems. Setting specific, realistic, and achievable goals is essential. By breaking down our larger goals into smaller, manageable tasks, we can celebrate milestones more frequently, keeping our motivation high. Additionally, choosing rewards that align with our values and desires ensures their effectiveness. The anticipation of a well-deserved reward can serve as a powerful motivator during challenging times.

4.   Celebrating   Mindfully:
While celebrating milestones and rewards is crucial, it is equally important to approach these celebrations mindfully. We should avoid excessive self-indulgence that may derail our progress or compromise our self-discipline. Instead, we must find a balance between celebration and maintaining our focus. Mindful celebrations allow us to fully embrace and appreciate our achievements while staying committed to our long-term goals.

Conclusion:
In the pursuit of self-discipline, celebrating milestones and rewards plays a vital role. By acknowledging our progress and rewarding ourselves along the way, we reinforce positive habits, maintain momentum, and cultivate a mindset of success. Mindful celebrations

not only provide well-deserved breaks but also fuel our motivation to continue striving towards our goals. So, let us embrace the power of celebrating milestones and rewards on our journey to transforming our habits and mindset.

Subchapter: Celebrating Milestones and Rewards

Introduction:
In our journey towards self-discipline, it is important to acknowledge and celebrate the milestones we achieve along the way. Recognizing and rewarding ourselves for small victories is a powerful motivator that helps to reinforce positive habits and mindset. In this subchapter, we will explore the significance of celebrating milestones and learn effective ways to reward ourselves on our path to self-discipline.

Acknowledging   Progress:
Self-discipline is a lifelong pursuit, and it is essential to acknowledge the progress we make. By recognizing even the smallest achievements, we can stay motivated and inspired to continue pushing forward. Celebrating milestones allows us to reflect on how far we have come, boosting our confidence and reinforcing our commitment to self-discipline.

The   Power   of   Rewards:
Rewards play a pivotal role in reinforcing positive behavior. When we reward ourselves, our brain releases dopamine, a neurotransmitter associated with pleasure and motivation. By linking rewards to milestones, we create a positive association with our efforts, making it easier to stay disciplined in the long run.

Effective Ways to Celebrate Milestones and Rewards: 1. Personal Reflection: Take a moment to reflect on your achievements. Write down the milestones you have reached and the challenges you have overcome. Acknowledge the efforts you put into your journey and the progress you have made.

2. Treat Yourself: Celebrate milestones by giving yourself a small treat. It could be something as simple as enjoying your favorite dessert, buying a new book, or taking a day off to relax and recharge. The key is to choose a reward that aligns with your values and brings you joy.

3. Share Your Success: Celebrating milestones with others can be a powerful experience. Share your achievements with friends, family, or a supportive community. Their encouragement and acknowledgment will further reinforce your commitment to self-discipline.

4. Set New Goals: Celebrating milestones is not just about looking back; it is also an opportunity to set new goals. Use this time to reflect on what you have learned and how you can continue to grow. Set new challenges that push you outside your comfort zone, ensuring a continuous cycle of growth and self-discipline.

Conclusion:
Celebrating milestones and rewarding ourselves along the journey of self-discipline is crucial in maintaining motivation and sustaining positive habits. By acknowledging our progress, we build confidence and strengthen our commitment to personal growth. Remember, celebrating milestones is not only about looking back but also about setting new goals and pushing ourselves to new heights. Embrace the

power of rewards, enjoy the journey, and watch yourself transform into the best version of yourself through the power of self-discipline.

In our journey towards self-discipline, it is essential to acknowledge and celebrate the milestones we achieve along the way. These milestones serve as markers of progress, reminding us of how far we have come and motivating us to keep pushing forward. They also provide an opportunity for us to reward ourselves for our hard work and dedication.

When we set goals for ourselves, whether big or small, it is crucial to establish a system of rewards. Rewards act as powerful incentives, reinforcing positive behavior and helping us stay motivated. They can come in various forms, depending on our preferences and what brings us joy. It could be something as simple as treating ourselves to our favorite meal, indulging in a spa day, or even planning a weekend getaway.

The key to effective rewards is to ensure they align with our goals and values. For instance, if your goal is to improve your physical fitness, a reward such as buying new workout clothes or investing in a gym membership would be appropriate. On the other hand, if your focus is on personal development, a reward like attending a seminar or purchasing a new book that aligns with your interests would be more fitting.

While rewards play a significant role in celebrating milestones, it is equally important to acknowledge the milestones themselves. By recognizing our accomplishments, we reinforce the positive habits and mindset we have cultivated through self-discipline. This recognition can be done through various means, such as sharing our achievements with loved ones, journaling about our progress, or even treating ourselves to a small celebration.

Celebrating milestones not only boosts our self-esteem but also reinforces the belief that we are capable of achieving our goals. It serves as a reminder that self-discipline is not just about denying ourselves of certain things but also about experiencing the joy and satisfaction that comes from accomplishing what we set out to do.

As we celebrate milestones and reward ourselves, it is important to remember that self-discipline is an ongoing journey. It is not a destination but a way of life. So, while it is crucial to acknowledge our achievements, we must also remain focused on our long-term goals and continue to cultivate self-discipline in all areas of our lives.

In conclusion, celebrating milestones and rewarding ourselves are vital components of our self-discipline journey. They provide the necessary motivation, reinforcement, and joy that keep us on track towards achieving our goals. So, let us take the time to acknowledge our progress, celebrate our achievements, and treat ourselves along the way. Remember, self-discipline is not about depriving ourselves, but rather about creating a life of purpose and fulfillment.

Adjusting Strategies for Continuous Improvement

In the journey towards achieving self-discipline, it is essential to understand that our strategies need to evolve and adapt continuously. Just like a well-oiled machine, our habits and mindset require regular adjustments to ensure continuous improvement. This subchapter explores the importance of adjusting strategies and provides valuable insights on how to do so effectively.

One of the key aspects of self-discipline is the ability to recognize when our strategies are not yielding the desired results. It is crucial to develop a keen sense of self-awareness and be open to making necessary changes. This involves evaluating our habits, mindset, and overall approach to self-discipline regularly. By actively monitoring our progress, we can identify areas that require improvement and adjust our strategies accordingly.

To adjust our strategies effectively, it is vital to set specific and measurable goals. Without clear objectives, it becomes challenging to determine whether our strategies are working or not. By defining what we want to achieve, we can evaluate and adjust our strategies based on the outcome. This allows us to stay focused and motivated while making necessary changes to ensure continuous improvement.

Flexibility is another key factor when it comes to adjusting strategies. We must be open to trying new approaches and techniques. What worked before may not work now, and it is crucial to embrace change. By exploring new strategies, we not only expand our knowledge and skills but also increase our chances of finding more effective methods of self-discipline.

Additionally, seeking feedback and learning from others is invaluable in adjusting our strategies. Surrounding ourselves with a supportive community or mentor who can provide constructive criticism and guidance can significantly accelerate our progress. They can offer fresh perspectives and insights, helping us identify blind spots and areas that need improvement. By being receptive to feedback, we can make the necessary adjustments to our strategies and continue growing.

Lastly, adjusting strategies for continuous improvement requires patience and perseverance. Change takes time, and setbacks are a natural part of the process. It is important to remain resilient and not get discouraged by temporary failures. Instead, view them as opportunities for learning and adjust strategies accordingly.

In conclusion, adjusting strategies for continuous improvement is a fundamental element of self-discipline. By regularly evaluating our progress, setting specific goals, remaining flexible, seeking feedback, and staying resilient, we can adapt our strategies effectively. Remember, self-discipline is a lifelong journey, and adjusting strategies along the way ensures that we continue to grow, evolve, and become the best version of ourselves.

In the pursuit of self-discipline, it is crucial to understand that the journey is not a linear path. It is a continuous process that requires constant adjustment and fine-tuning of strategies. As we strive to transform our habits and mindset, it is essential to embrace the concept of continuous improvement.

To embark on this journey, we must first acknowledge that self-discipline is not a destination but rather a lifelong commitment. It requires adaptability and the willingness to adjust our strategies along the way. By doing so, we can propel ourselves towards personal growth and success.

One effective strategy for continuous improvement is to regularly evaluate our progress. This involves reflecting on our habits and actions, identifying areas of improvement, and making necessary adjustments. By conducting self-assessments, we can pinpoint our strengths and weaknesses, enabling us to enhance our self-discipline in specific areas.

Moreover, it is vital to set realistic and achievable goals. By breaking down larger goals into smaller, manageable tasks, we can maintain motivation and a sense of accomplishment. As we progress, we can reassess our goals, making adjustments if necessary to ensure they remain aligned with our evolving aspirations.

Another crucial aspect of continuous improvement is embracing failure and setbacks as opportunities for growth. Instead of being discouraged by setbacks, we should view them as valuable learning experiences. By analyzing our failures, we gain insights into what went wrong and how we can improve moving forward. Embracing a growth mindset allows us to see setbacks as stepping stones towards success.

In addition, seeking feedback and guidance from mentors or accountability partners can significantly contribute to our continuous improvement journey. Surrounding ourselves with individuals who share similar goals and values can provide valuable insights and support. Their perspectives can help us identify blind spots, suggest alternative strategies, and provide ongoing motivation.

Ultimately, adjusting strategies for continuous improvement requires a commitment to self-reflection, setting realistic goals, embracing failure, and seeking support from others. By adopting these practices, we can enhance our self-discipline and continue to grow as individuals.

Whether you are just starting on your self-discipline journey or have been working on it for a while, remember that it is an ongoing process. Embrace the idea of continuous improvement, adjust your strategies as needed, and celebrate the progress you make along the way. With dedication, perseverance, and a growth mindset, you can unleash the power of self-discipline and transform your habits and mindset for lasting success.

Continuous improvement is the key to personal growth and success in every aspect of life. It is the process of making incremental changes and adjustments to your strategies and habits to achieve better results. In the realm of self-discipline, adjusting strategies for continuous improvement is crucial to maintaining a strong mindset and achieving your goals.

One of the first steps in adjusting strategies for continuous improvement is to regularly evaluate your progress. Take the time to reflect on your current habits and strategies and assess whether they are helping you move closer to your goals or if they need to be adjusted. This self-reflection allows you to identify areas for improvement and make necessary changes.

Once you have identified areas that need improvement, it's essential to develop a plan for adjustment. This plan should include specific actions that you will take to address the areas of weakness. For example, if you struggle with procrastination, you might establish a new routine that includes prioritizing tasks and setting specific deadlines.

Another important aspect of adjusting strategies for continuous improvement is seeking feedback from others. Surround yourself with individuals who support your goals and are willing to provide constructive criticism. Their insights can offer a fresh perspective and help you identify blind spots or areas where you may be falling short. Embrace feedback as an opportunity for growth and use it to refine your strategies.

Flexibility is also a key component of adjusting strategies for continuous improvement. Recognize that not all strategies will work for every person or situation. Be open to trying new approaches and be willing to adapt your strategies based on the results you are getting. Adjusting your strategies requires a willingness to step outside of your comfort zone and experiment with new methods.

Finally, adjusting strategies for continuous improvement requires patience and persistence. Change takes time, and setbacks are inevitable. However, maintaining a growth mindset and staying committed to your goals will ultimately lead to long-term success. Embrace the journey of self-discipline and view setbacks as opportunities to learn and grow.

In conclusion, adjusting strategies for continuous improvement is essential for anyone seeking to enhance their self-discipline. Regularly evaluating progress, developing a plan for adjustment, seeking feedback, embracing flexibility, and maintaining patience and persistence are all key factors in this process. By continuously refining your strategies, you can cultivate self-discipline and transform your habits and mindset, leading to personal growth and success in all areas of life.

Finding Inspiration and Motivation

In our journey towards self-discipline, there are bound to be moments when we feel unmotivated or lacking inspiration. It is during these times that we need to tap into our inner reserves and find ways to reignite our passion and drive. This subchapter aims to provide you with practical tips and strategies to help you find inspiration and motivation in your pursuit of self-discipline.

One of the most effective ways to find inspiration is by setting clear goals for yourself. When you have a clear vision of what you want to achieve, it becomes easier to stay motivated and focused. Take some time to identify your long-term goals and break them down into smaller, achievable milestones. By doing so, you create a roadmap that helps you stay on track and provides you with a sense of purpose.

Another powerful source of inspiration is surrounding yourself with like-minded individuals. Seek out a community or support group that shares your interest in self-discipline. Engaging with others who are on a similar journey can provide you with valuable insights, encouragement, and accountability. Additionally, reading books or listening to podcasts by influential individuals who have achieved self-discipline can also inspire and motivate you.

While external sources of inspiration are valuable, it is equally important to cultivate an internal source of motivation. Take some time to reflect on your personal values and beliefs. What drives you? What are your passions? Connecting with your inner self and aligning your actions with your values can create a strong sense of motivation and purpose.

In moments of low motivation, it can be helpful to revisit your past successes. Remind yourself of the times when you overcame challenges and achieved your goals. Remembering your past victories can reignite your belief in yourself and your ability to succeed.

Lastly, make sure to take care of your physical and mental well-being. Engage in activities that bring you joy and relaxation. Exercise regularly, eat a balanced diet, and get enough sleep. When your body and mind are healthy, you are more likely to stay motivated and inspired.

In conclusion, finding inspiration and motivation is crucial for maintaining self-discipline. Set clear goals, surround yourself with supportive individuals, connect with your inner self, revisit past successes, and take care of your well-being. By incorporating these strategies into your life, you can stay inspired, motivated, and committed to your journey of self-discipline.

In the journey of self-discipline, it is crucial to find inspiration and motivation to keep moving forward. Whether you are a student, professional, or a homemaker, self-discipline is a valuable trait that can transform your habits and mindset. It empowers you to take control of your life and achieve your goals. However, maintaining self-discipline can be challenging at times, and that's when you need to tap into your inner well of inspiration and motivation.

So how do you find that spark that ignites your drive to stay disciplined? Here are a few strategies that can help:

1. Define your purpose: Understanding why you want to develop self-discipline is the first step. What are your goals? What do you want to

achieve? Identifying your purpose will provide you with a clear direction and a compelling reason to stay disciplined.

2. Seek inspiration from others: Look for individuals who have achieved what you aspire to accomplish. Read their success stories, watch interviews, or attend seminars where they share their experiences. Their journey can serve as a source of inspiration, reminding you that if they can do it, so can you.

3. Surround yourself with positive influences: Surrounding yourself with like-minded individuals who prioritize self-discipline can be immensely beneficial. Join communities, forums, or social media groups where you can connect with people who share similar goals. Their support and encouragement can help you stay motivated on your self-discipline journey.

4. Create a vision board: Visualize your goals and dreams by creating a vision board. Cut out pictures or write down your aspirations and display them in a prominent place. This visual reminder will keep you focused and inspire you to work towards your objectives.

5. Break your goals into smaller milestones: Sometimes, the enormity of a goal can be overwhelming, leading to a lack of motivation. Break your goals into smaller, achievable milestones. Celebrate each milestone you achieve, as it will fuel your motivation to keep going.

6. Embrace failure as a learning opportunity: It's natural to face setbacks on your self-discipline journey. However, rather than letting failures demotivate you, use them as learning opportunities. Analyze what went wrong, make necessary adjustments, and get back on track with renewed determination.

Remember, finding inspiration and motivation is a continuous process. It requires effort and dedication to keep the fire burning. By incorporating these strategies into your life, you can tap into your inner strength and unleash the power of self-discipline, transforming your habits and mindset. So, embrace the journey, stay inspired, and let your self-discipline guide you towards a fulfilling and successful life.

In our journey towards self-discipline, finding inspiration and motivation is crucial. Without these driving forces, it becomes challenging to stay focused, maintain good habits, and achieve our goals. Whether you are striving for personal growth, career success, or overall well-being, the following strategies will help you tap into your inner motivation and find inspiration to fuel your self-discipline.

1. Define Your Why: Understanding your purpose and reasons behind your goals can provide a powerful source of motivation. Take the time to clarify why you want to develop self-discipline and what you hope to achieve. Write down your goals and revisit them regularly to stay connected to your why.

2. Surround Yourself with Positive Influences: Seek out individuals who inspire and motivate you. Surrounding yourself with like-minded people who have similar aspirations can boost your motivation and provide the necessary support when challenges arise. Joining communities, attending workshops, or finding mentors can significantly impact your self-discipline journey.

3. Seek Inspiration from Success Stories: Reading about the achievements of others who have overcome obstacles and reached

their goals can ignite inspiration within you. Look for biographies, articles, or TED Talks that resonate with your interests and goals. Learning from these success stories can offer valuable insights and demonstrate that you too can overcome any hurdles on your path to self-discipline.

4. Visualize Your Success: Close your eyes and imagine yourself achieving your goals. Visualizing success can intensify your motivation and make your aspirations feel more attainable. Create a vision board or journal where you can capture your dreams and revisit them regularly. Visual reminders of your goals can keep you focused and inspired.

5. Celebrate Small Wins: Acknowledging and celebrating your progress along the way can boost your motivation. Break down your goals into smaller, manageable steps, and reward yourself when you achieve them. By recognizing your efforts, you'll feel encouraged to continue working towards your larger objectives.

6. Embrace Failure as a Learning Opportunity: Failure is an inevitable part of any journey towards self-discipline. Instead of letting setbacks demotivate you, view them as opportunities for growth and learning. Analyze what went wrong, make adjustments, and keep pushing forward. Remember, failure is not the end; it's a stepping stone towards success.

Finding inspiration and motivation is an ongoing process. Discover what works best for you and incorporate these strategies into your daily life. By staying motivated and inspired, you will unlock the power of self-discipline and transform your habits and mindset for a more fulfilling and successful life.

Creating a Sustainable Self-Discipline Routine

In today's fast-paced world, self-discipline is a crucial skill that can lead to personal and professional success. Whether you want to improve your health, excel in your career, or achieve personal goals, self-discipline is the key to unlocking your full potential. However, developing self-discipline is not always easy. It requires dedication, commitment, and the establishment of a sustainable routine.

One of the first steps in creating a sustainable self-discipline routine is to identify your goals. What are the areas of your life where you want to exercise more self-discipline? Is it in your work habits, fitness routine, or personal relationships? Once you have a clear understanding of your goals, you can start building a routine that supports your aspirations.

To create a sustainable routine, it's essential to start small. Begin by incorporating small acts of self-discipline into your daily life. For example, if your goal is to exercise regularly, commit to a short workout session every morning. As you consistently practice this routine, you can gradually increase the duration and intensity of your workouts. By starting small and gradually building up, you'll be more likely to stick with your routine in the long term.

Another important aspect of creating a sustainable self-discipline routine is to eliminate distractions and create a conducive environment. Identify the factors that hinder your self-discipline, whether it's excessive screen time, a cluttered workspace, or negative influences. Take proactive steps to eliminate or minimize these distractions and create an environment that supports your self-discipline goals.

Additionally, it's crucial to prioritize self-care and rest. Pushing yourself too hard without adequate rest can lead to burnout and make it difficult to maintain a sustainable routine. Make sure to schedule regular breaks, get enough sleep, and engage in activities that help you relax and rejuvenate. By taking care of yourself, you'll have the energy and mental clarity to stay focused and disciplined.

Lastly, accountability is key when it comes to sustaining self-discipline. Find an accountability partner or join a community of like-minded individuals who can support and motivate you on your journey. Share your goals, progress, and challenges with them to stay on track and receive valuable feedback.

In conclusion, creating a sustainable self-discipline routine requires setting clear goals, starting small, eliminating distractions, prioritizing self-care, and seeking accountability. By incorporating these strategies into your daily life, you can develop the self-discipline necessary to transform your habits and mindset, ultimately leading to personal growth and success. Remember, self-discipline is a lifelong journey, so be patient and persistent in your efforts.

In today's fast-paced world, self-discipline has become more important than ever. It is the key to achieving success, personal growth, and overall fulfillment. However, many people struggle to maintain a consistent self-discipline routine, often falling into the trap of procrastination or easily getting distracted. In this subchapter, we will explore strategies and techniques to help you create a sustainable self-discipline routine that will empower you to transform your habits and mindset.

1. Define Your Purpose: The first step in creating a sustainable self-discipline routine is to identify your purpose. Ask yourself: What do I want to achieve? What are my long-term goals? Understanding your purpose will provide you with the motivation and the drive to stay disciplined.

2. Set Clear, Attainable Goals: Break down your long-term goals into smaller, manageable tasks. Set clear, attainable goals for yourself. These smaller goals will give you a sense of progress and accomplishment, boosting your self-discipline.

3. Establish a Routine: Develop a daily routine that supports your goals. Determine the most productive time of the day for you and allocate it to your most important tasks. By establishing a routine, you create a sense of structure and discipline in your life.

4. Prioritize and Focus: Learn to prioritize your tasks and eliminate distractions. Focus on the most important tasks first, and don't let minor distractions divert your attention. Use time management techniques such as the Pomodoro Technique to enhance your focus and concentration.

5. Develop Self-Awareness: Cultivate self-awareness to understand your strengths and weaknesses. Identify the habits and behaviors that hinder your self-discipline and work on ways to overcome them. This could involve seeking support from mentors or joining accountability groups.

6. Practice Mindfulness: Incorporate mindfulness practices into your routine. Mindfulness helps you stay present and aware of your thoughts and actions, enabling you to make conscious choices aligned with your goals. Meditation, deep breathing exercises, or journaling can be effective mindfulness tools.

7. Celebrate Progress: Celebrate your achievements along the way. Rewarding yourself for small milestones will reinforce your self-discipline and keep you motivated to continue. This could be treating yourself to something you enjoy or taking a break to recharge.

Remember, creating a sustainable self-discipline routine is a journey. It requires consistent effort and commitment. By implementing these strategies and techniques, you can develop the self-discipline necessary to transform your habits and mindset, ultimately leading to a more fulfilling and successful life. Start today and embrace the power of self-discipline.

Self-discipline is the key to achieving success and realizing your full potential. It is the ability to control your thoughts, emotions, and actions in order to stay focused on your goals and make consistent progress towards them. However, developing self-discipline is not an easy task. It requires effort, commitment, and the establishment of a sustainable routine that supports your self-discipline journey.

In this subchapter, we will explore the essential steps to creating a sustainable self-discipline routine that can transform your habits and mindset. These steps are applicable to everyone, regardless of their current level of self-discipline. Let's dive in.

1. Define Your Goals: Start by clearly defining your short-term and long-term goals. Be specific and make them measurable. This will provide you with a clear direction and a purpose for developing self-discipline.

2. Prioritize: Determine which goals are most important to you and prioritize them accordingly. By focusing on a few key goals, you can avoid spreading yourself too thin and increase your chances of success.

3. Create a Daily Schedule: Design a daily schedule that includes designated time blocks for working towards your goals. Break down your tasks into manageable chunks and allocate specific time slots for each. Stick to this schedule as much as possible to develop consistency.

4. Develop Positive Habits: Identify habits that align with your goals and incorporate them into your routine. For example, if your goal is to improve your physical fitness, make it a habit to exercise for 30 minutes every morning. Consistently practicing positive habits will strengthen your self-discipline muscles.

5. Eliminate Distractions: Identify the distractions that hinder your progress and take proactive steps to eliminate or minimize them. This could involve turning off notifications on your phone, creating a designated workspace, or establishing boundaries with others.

6. Practice Mindfulness and Reflection: Take time each day to practice mindfulness and reflect on your progress. This will help you stay present, focused, and aware of any adjustments you need to make to your routine.

7. Celebrate Small Wins: Acknowledge and celebrate your accomplishments along the way. Rewarding yourself for achieving milestones, no matter how small, will reinforce positive behavior and motivate you to continue on your self-discipline journey.

Remember, developing self-discipline is a gradual process. It requires patience, perseverance, and the willingness to adapt as you learn more about yourself. By following these steps and creating a sustainable self-discipline routine, you will be well on your way to transforming your habits and mindset, empowering yourself to achieve the success you desire.

Chapter 8: Transforming Your Habits and Mindset

Reinforcing Positive Habits and Breaking Bad Ones

Introduction:

In our journey towards personal growth and success, the role of self-discipline cannot be overstated. It is the cornerstone upon which we build a life of purpose, achievement, and fulfillment. One of the key aspects of self-discipline is the ability to reinforce positive habits while simultaneously breaking bad ones. In this subchapter, we will explore effective strategies to strengthen our self-discipline, empowering us to transform our habits and mindset.

Understanding the Power of Habits:

Habits are deeply ingrained patterns of behavior that shape our lives. They can either propel us towards success or hold us back. Recognizing the power of habits is the first step towards taking control of our lives. By understanding how habits are formed and maintained, we can leverage this knowledge to reinforce positive habits and eliminate negative ones.

Creating Positive Habits:

To reinforce positive habits, it is essential to start small and focus on consistency. Begin by identifying one habit that aligns with your goals and values. Then, devise a plan that includes specific actions and a timeline. By consistently taking small steps towards the desired habit, you will gradually solidify it into your routine. Additionally, employing positive reinforcement, such as rewards or tracking progress, can provide the motivation needed to maintain these habits.

Breaking Bad Habits:

Breaking bad habits requires self-awareness, commitment, and resilience. Start by identifying the triggers that lead to the habit and explore alternative behaviors to replace it. For example, if you tend to reach for unhealthy snacks when stressed, find healthier alternatives like going for a walk or practicing deep breathing exercises. Additionally, surrounding yourself with a supportive network and seeking accountability can greatly enhance your chances of success.

The Role of Mindset:

Cultivating a growth mindset is crucial when reinforcing positive habits and breaking bad ones. Embrace the belief that change is possible and setbacks are opportunities for learning. Rather than viewing failures as a reflection of your worth, see them as stepping stones towards improvement. By adopting a positive and resilient mindset, you will be better equipped to face challenges and stay committed to your goals.

Conclusion:

Reinforcing positive habits and breaking bad ones is a lifelong journey that requires self-discipline, commitment, and a growth mindset. By understanding the power of habits, creating a plan, and utilizing positive reinforcement, you can reinforce positive behaviors and eliminate negative ones. Remember that change takes time and effort, but with persistence and a belief in your ability to change, you can transform your habits and mindset for a more fulfilling and successful life.

In the journey of personal growth and self-improvement, one of the key elements that can make or break your success is the power of self-discipline. It is the ability to reinforce positive habits and break free from the clutches of bad ones that truly defines our character and determines our achievements.

Developing self-discipline is not an overnight process; it requires consistent effort and dedication. However, the rewards that come from mastering this skill are truly remarkable. By reinforcing positive habits, we can create a solid foundation for success in all areas of life, while simultaneously breaking bad habits that hinder our progress.

To reinforce positive habits, it is essential to first identify the habits that align with our goals and values. These habits could include regular exercise, healthy eating, practicing gratitude, or consistently working towards our aspirations. Once we have identified these habits, we can begin incorporating them into our daily routines.

One effective strategy to reinforce positive habits is through the power of repetition. By consistently engaging in these habits, we create neural pathways in our brain that make them easier to perform over time. This repetition helps to solidify these habits as a part of our lifestyle, making them effortless and automatic.

Additionally, it is crucial to celebrate small victories along the way to reinforce positive habits. By acknowledging and rewarding ourselves for consistently practicing these habits, we can create a positive association in our minds. This positive reinforcement further motivates us to continue our progress and strengthens our self-discipline.

On the other hand, breaking bad habits requires a different approach. Firstly, it is crucial to identify the triggers and underlying reasons behind these habits. Once we are aware of the factors that lead us to engage in these negative behaviors, we can begin to develop strategies to overcome them.

Replacing bad habits with healthier alternatives is an effective way to break free from their grasp. For example, if we have a habit of stress-eating, we can replace it with a habit of going for a walk or practicing deep breathing exercises when we feel overwhelmed. By consciously choosing a healthier alternative, we can rewire our brain and gradually eliminate the bad habit.

Lastly, it is important to surround ourselves with a supportive environment that encourages positive habits and discourages bad ones. By seeking the company of like-minded individuals who prioritize self-discipline, we can draw inspiration and motivation from their habits and mindset.

In conclusion, reinforcing positive habits and breaking bad ones are fundamental aspects of self-discipline. By consistently practicing positive habits, celebrating small wins, and replacing bad habits with healthier alternatives, we can transform our habits and mindset. With self-discipline as our guiding force, we can unlock our true potential and achieve success in every aspect of our lives.

Self-discipline is a powerful tool that can transform our habits and mindset, leading us towards a more fulfilling and successful life. In this subchapter, we will delve into the strategies and techniques for reinforcing positive habits and breaking bad ones. Whether you are struggling with procrastination, unhealthy habits, or lack of focus, these principles can be applied by anyone to cultivate self-discipline.

To reinforce positive habits, the first step is to identify the habits you wish to cultivate. Start with small, achievable goals and build upon them gradually. Consistency is key, so create a routine and stick to it. By doing so, you will wire your brain to automate these habits, making them more ingrained and easier to maintain.

Accountability is another crucial aspect of reinforcing positive habits. Find an accountability partner, someone who will hold you responsible for your actions and progress. This could be a friend, family member, or even a coach. Regular check-ins and feedback will help you stay on track and push through challenges.

Rewarding yourself for achieving your desired habits is an effective way to reinforce positive behavior. Celebrate your accomplishments, no matter how small, and acknowledge the progress you have made. This will motivate you to continue on your journey towards self-discipline.

Breaking bad habits requires a different approach. Firstly, identify the triggers and cues that lead to the unwanted behavior. This could be certain situations, emotions, or people. By recognizing these triggers, you can develop alternative responses or strategies to counteract them.

Replacing bad habits with healthier alternatives is an effective way to break free from destructive patterns. For example, if you find yourself reaching for unhealthy snacks when stressed, replace them with nutritious options or find alternative ways to manage stress, such as exercise or meditation.

Self-awareness is essential in breaking bad habits. Pay attention to the negative consequences of your actions and reflect on how they impact your life. By understanding the root causes and consequences, you can develop a stronger motivation to change.

Lastly, be patient and kind with yourself throughout this process. Breaking bad habits and reinforcing positive ones takes time and effort. There will be setbacks and challenges along the way, but remember that each day is a new opportunity to make better choices.

In conclusion, self-discipline can be cultivated by reinforcing positive habits and breaking bad ones. By implementing the strategies mentioned above, anyone can develop the self-discipline necessary for personal growth and success. Remember, it is never too late to start transforming your habits and mindset.

Embracing Change and Adaptability

Change is an inevitable part of life. Whether we like it or not, it is constantly happening around us. The ability to adapt to these changes is a crucial skill that can make all the difference in our personal and professional lives. In the realm of self-discipline, embracing change and adaptability is an essential mindset to cultivate.

One of the first steps in embracing change is accepting that it is a natural and necessary part of growth. Change can be scary and uncomfortable, but it is often through these challenging moments that we find new opportunities for personal development. By acknowledging that change is an opportunity for growth, we can shift our perspective and approach it with an open mind.

To embrace change effectively, it is important to develop a flexible mindset. This means being willing to let go of old habits, routines, and beliefs that no longer serve us. It requires us to be open to new ideas, perspectives, and ways of doing things. By being flexible, we can adapt to new situations and take advantage of the opportunities that come our way.

Another aspect of embracing change is being proactive rather than reactive. Instead of resisting or avoiding change, we should actively seek out ways to adapt and improve. This may involve seeking new knowledge and skills, networking with like-minded individuals, or even taking calculated risks. By being proactive, we can stay ahead of the game and navigate through change more smoothly.

Embracing change and adaptability also requires a certain level of self-discipline. It takes effort and commitment to let go of old habits and embrace new ones. It is important to stay focused on our goals and take consistent action towards them, even in the face of change. This requires self-awareness and self-control, as well as the ability to stay motivated and resilient.

In conclusion, embracing change and adaptability is a crucial aspect of self-discipline. By cultivating a flexible mindset, being proactive, and maintaining self-discipline, we can navigate through change with ease and make the most of the opportunities that come our way. So, let us embrace change as a catalyst for growth and transformation, and develop the adaptability needed to thrive in an ever-changing world.

Change is the only constant in life. In today's fast-paced and ever-evolving world, the ability to embrace change and adapt is more important than ever before. This subchapter will explore the significance of change and how developing self-discipline can help individuals navigate through these transitions successfully.

Change can be intimidating and unsettling for many people. It disrupts routines, challenges comfort zones, and requires individuals to step outside of their familiar territory. However, change also presents opportunities for growth, learning, and personal development. By embracing change, individuals open themselves up to new possibilities and experiences that can ultimately lead to a more fulfilling life.

Adaptability is a fundamental trait of successful individuals. Those who possess it can quickly adjust their mindset, behaviors, and strategies to align with new circumstances. They embrace change as an opportunity for growth rather than a threat to their stability.

Adaptability enables individuals to face challenges head-on, overcome obstacles, and thrive in unpredictable environments.

Developing self-discipline is crucial in cultivating adaptability. Self-discipline empowers individuals to take charge of their actions and responses to change. It helps them stay focused, motivated, and resilient during uncertain times. With self-discipline, individuals can maintain a proactive approach to change, rather than being reactive or overwhelmed by it.

One of the keys to embracing change and adaptability is cultivating a growth mindset. A growth mindset allows individuals to see change as an opportunity for self-improvement and progress. It encourages continuous learning, flexibility, and openness to new ideas. By adopting a growth mindset, individuals become more resilient and adaptable in the face of change.

In this subchapter, we will explore practical strategies and techniques to develop self-discipline and embrace change. We will discuss the importance of setting clear goals, maintaining focus, and developing a positive attitude towards change. We will also provide tips on managing stress, overcoming resistance to change, and developing a growth mindset.

In conclusion, embracing change and adaptability is essential for personal growth and success in today's rapidly changing world. By developing self-discipline and adopting a growth mindset, individuals can navigate through change with grace and resilience. This subchapter aims to equip readers with the tools and knowledge necessary to embrace change as an opportunity for personal transformation. Whether you are a student, professional, or simply someone seeking personal growth, embracing change and adaptability will empower you to thrive in the face of uncertainty.

Change is inevitable in life. It is a constant force that shapes our experiences, challenges us, and pushes us to grow. In today's fast-paced world, where everything seems to be constantly evolving, the ability to adapt becomes crucial for success. This subchapter, "Embracing Change and Adaptability," delves into the importance of self-discipline in navigating through life's changes and how it can transform our mindset.

Change can be intimidating and overwhelming for many individuals. It disrupts routines, introduces uncertainty, and often pushes us out of our comfort zones. However, those who embrace change and adapt to new circumstances are the ones who thrive in both personal and professional aspects of life. This subchapter aims to empower readers to develop the self-discipline necessary to embrace change with open arms.

The first step in embracing change is to cultivate a growth mindset. This mindset allows us to view challenges and setbacks as opportunities for learning and growth. By adopting a positive attitude and embracing change as a chance for personal development, we can navigate through life's transitions with resilience and determination.

Next, the subchapter explores the importance of self-discipline in adapting to change. It emphasizes that self-discipline is not about restricting ourselves or following strict rules, but rather about taking control of our actions and responses. By practicing self-discipline, we can proactively adapt to change, rather than being passive recipients of it.

The subchapter provides practical strategies and techniques to develop self-discipline in the face of change. It discusses the power of setting clear goals, managing time effectively, and focusing on priorities. It also highlights the importance of self-reflection and self-awareness in identifying areas for improvement and embracing change.

Moreover, the subchapter emphasizes the significance of embracing change in our personal and professional lives. It showcases real-life examples of individuals who have embraced change and achieved remarkable success. It inspires readers to step out of their comfort zones, embrace uncertainty, and pursue their goals with unwavering determination.

In conclusion, "Embracing Change and Adaptability" is a subchapter that explores the transformative power of self-discipline in navigating through life's changes. It provides practical strategies and insights to develop a growth mindset, embrace change, and adapt to new circumstances. Whether you are an individual seeking personal growth or a professional aiming for success, the lessons from this subchapter will empower you to face change with confidence and determination.

Developing Self-Awareness and Mindfulness

In our fast-paced and chaotic world, self-discipline has become a crucial quality for success and personal growth. However, before embarking on the journey of self-discipline, it is essential to develop self-awareness and mindfulness. These two foundational aspects lay the groundwork for building a strong and resilient mindset that will support your self-discipline efforts.

Self-awareness is the ability to recognize and understand one's thoughts, emotions, and behaviors. It involves being in tune with our inner selves and being honest about our strengths, weaknesses, and limitations. By cultivating self-awareness, we gain a deeper understanding of our motivations, triggers, and patterns of behavior. This awareness enables us to make conscious choices and take deliberate actions that align with our long-term goals and values.

Mindfulness complements self-awareness by bringing our attention to the present moment. It involves being fully present and engaged in whatever we are doing, without judgment or attachment to the outcome. Mindfulness helps us develop a non-reactive state of mind, allowing us to respond to situations with clarity and composure instead of reacting impulsively. By practicing mindfulness, we cultivate a calm and focused mind, which is essential for sustaining self-discipline in the face of challenges and distractions.

To develop self-awareness and mindfulness, it is important to engage in daily practices that foster these qualities. Incorporating meditation into your routine can be immensely beneficial. Start with just a few minutes a day, gradually increasing the duration as you become more comfortable. Meditation helps to quiet the mind, enhances self-awareness, and cultivates mindfulness.

Journaling is another powerful tool for self-reflection and self-awareness. Take a few minutes each day to write down your thoughts, emotions, and experiences. By observing your patterns and reactions, you gain valuable insights into your inner world.

Engaging in activities that promote mindfulness, such as yoga or mindful walking, can also be helpful. These practices encourage you to focus on your body and breath, bringing your attention to the present moment.

By developing self-awareness and mindfulness, you will not only enhance your self-disciplinc but also lead a more fulfilling and purposeful life. Understanding yourself on a deeper level and being fully present in each moment empowers you to make conscious choices that align with your goals and values. So, take the time to cultivate self-awareness and mindfulness, and witness the transformation it brings to your mindset and habits.

In the fast-paced world we live in, where distractions are abundant and demands are constant, it can be easy to lose sight of ourselves and our goals. However, self-discipline requires a deeper understanding of who we are and what drives us. This is where the power of self-awareness and mindfulness comes into play.

Self-awareness is the foundation upon which self-discipline is built. It involves having a clear understanding of our strengths, weaknesses, and values. By becoming more self-aware, we can identify the areas in our lives that need improvement and focus our efforts on developing self-discipline in those areas.

One way to cultivate self-awareness is through reflection. Taking the time to pause and reflect on our thoughts, emotions, and actions allows us to gain insights into ourselves. Journaling, meditation, or even having regular conversations with trusted friends or mentors can help us uncover patterns and triggers that may hinder our self-discipline.

Mindfulness, on the other hand, involves being fully present in the moment and paying attention to our thoughts, emotions, and physical sensations without judgment. It helps us become more aware of our automatic reactions and enables us to respond consciously rather than react impulsively.

Practicing mindfulness can be as simple as taking a few minutes each day to focus on our breath or engaging in activities that bring us joy and calmness. By incorporating mindfulness into our daily routines, we can enhance our self-discipline by being more intentional and purposeful in our actions.

Developing self-awareness and mindfulness also requires cultivating patience and compassion towards ourselves. It is important to remember that self-discipline is a journey, and setbacks are inevitable. By practicing self-compassion, we can learn from our mistakes, forgive ourselves, and continue to grow.

In the book "The Power of Self-Discipline: Transforming Your Habits and Mindset," readers will discover practical strategies and exercises to develop self-awareness and mindfulness. Through real-life examples and research-backed techniques, the book empowers individuals from all walks of life to harness their inner strength and cultivate self-discipline.

Whether you are a student striving to improve your study habits, an entrepreneur aiming to build a successful business, or simply someone wanting to lead a more fulfilling life, this subchapter will provide you with the tools and knowledge necessary to develop self-awareness and mindfulness as a foundation for self-discipline.

Remember, self-discipline is not about perfection, but rather progress. By embracing self-awareness and mindfulness, you will embark on a transformative journey towards a more disciplined and purposeful life.

In the pursuit of self-discipline, it is crucial to develop self awareness and mindfulness. These two qualities act as the foundation upon which we can build a strong and unwavering discipline. By cultivating self-awareness, we gain insight into our thoughts, emotions, and behaviors, allowing us to make conscious choices and take control of our lives.

Self-awareness begins with observing ourselves without judgment. It involves paying attention to our thoughts, feelings, and reactions in various situations. By doing so, we can identify patterns and triggers that lead to unproductive or self-sabotaging behaviors. This awareness empowers us to make proactive changes and break free from negative cycles.

Moreover, mindfulness complements self-awareness by teaching us to live in the present moment. Often, our minds wander, dwelling on the past or worrying about the future. Mindfulness helps us redirect our focus to the present, enabling us to fully engage with our current tasks and experiences. By cultivating mindfulness, we develop a greater sense of clarity and concentration, which are essential for maintaining self-discipline.

To develop self-awareness and mindfulness, we can engage in various practices. Meditation, for example, allows us to train our minds to be more present and aware. By setting aside a few minutes each day to sit in silence and focus on our breath, we can cultivate a sense of calm and clarity that extends into our daily lives.

Another effective practice is journaling. By regularly writing down our thoughts and reflections, we gain insight into our emotions and behaviors. This practice helps us identify recurring patterns and understand the underlying reasons behind our actions. Journaling also serves as a therapeutic outlet, allowing us to release pent-up emotions and gain a fresh perspective on challenging situations.

Additionally, seeking feedback from trusted friends, family, or mentors can provide valuable insights into our blind spots. Others may notice patterns or behaviors that we are unaware of, helping us gain a more accurate understanding of ourselves. Constructive feedback allows us to grow and make positive changes, further enhancing our self-discipline.

In conclusion, developing self-awareness and mindfulness are essential for cultivating self-discipline. By becoming more aware of our thoughts, emotions, and behaviors, and by living in the present moment, we gain the power to make conscious choices and break free from unproductive habits. Through practices such as meditation, journaling, and seeking feedback, we can strengthen these qualities and transform our habits and mindset. Embracing self-awareness and mindfulness opens the doors to a life of empowered self-discipline, allowing us to achieve our goals and unlock our true potential.

Cultivating a Positive and Growth-Oriented Mindset

In today's fast-paced and competitive world, cultivating a positive and growth-oriented mindset is crucial for achieving success in all aspects of life. Whether you are striving to improve your career, relationships, or personal goals, having the right mindset can make all the difference. This subchapter explores the power of self-discipline in transforming your habits and mindset and provides practical tips for developing a positive and growth-oriented mindset.

Self-discipline is the foundation for cultivating a positive mindset. It is the ability to control your impulses, stay focused, and persevere in the face of challenges. By developing self-discipline, you can train your mind to think positively and approach obstacles as opportunities for growth. It allows you to overcome self-limiting beliefs and achieve your full potential.

One of the first steps in developing a positive mindset is to become aware of your thoughts and beliefs. Negative thoughts and self-doubt can hinder your progress and limit your potential. By consciously monitoring your thoughts and replacing negative ones with positive affirmations, you can rewire your brain for positivity. Practice gratitude daily, as it helps shift your focus towards the positive aspects of your life.

Another important aspect of cultivating a positive mindset is to embrace failure and setbacks as learning experiences. Instead of dwelling on past mistakes, view them as stepping stones towards growth and improvement. Understand that failure is a natural part of the learning process and an opportunity for personal development. By adopting this perspective, you can bounce back from setbacks stronger and more resilient than before.

A growth-oriented mindset is also characterized by a willingness to step out of your comfort zone. Embrace challenges and seek new opportunities for personal and professional growth. By pushing yourself beyond your limits, you will discover new abilities and talents that you never knew existed. Remember, growth happens outside of your comfort zone.

Finally, surround yourself with positive and like-minded individuals who support your growth journey. Seek out mentors and role models who can inspire and guide you. Join communities and networks that promote personal development and self-discipline. By surrounding yourself with positivity, you can reinforce your growth-oriented mindset and stay motivated on your path to success.

In conclusion, cultivating a positive and growth-oriented mindset is essential for achieving success in life. By developing self-discipline, embracing failure as a learning opportunity, stepping out of your comfort zone, and surrounding yourself with positivity, you can transform your habits and mindset. Remember, a positive mindset is not something you are born with; it is a skill that can be developed through practice and self-discipline.

In the journey of self-discipline, one of the most crucial aspects to master is developing a positive and growth-oriented mindset. The way we perceive ourselves, our abilities, and our potential directly influences our actions and outcomes. By cultivating a positive and growth-oriented mindset, we can unlock our true potential and achieve remarkable personal growth.

A positive mindset starts with self-belief. It is about acknowledging and appreciating our strengths, skills, and accomplishments. When we believe in ourselves, we become more resilient and motivated to overcome challenges. We understand that setbacks and failures are merely temporary roadblocks on the path to success. Embracing a positive mindset empowers us to stay focused and persistent, even when faced with adversity.

Another crucial element of a growth-oriented mindset is the willingness to learn and grow. It involves embracing challenges and seeing them as opportunities for personal development. Instead of being discouraged by failures, we view them as valuable learning experiences. By adopting a growth-oriented mindset, we understand that our abilities can be developed through dedication and effort. This mindset allows us to continuously improve ourselves, both personally and professionally.

To cultivate a positive and growth-oriented mindset, it is essential to surround ourselves with positive influences. This includes seeking out mentors, coaches, or like-minded individuals who encourage and inspire us. Their support and guidance can help us navigate challenging situations and push us to achieve new heights.

Additionally, practicing gratitude is a powerful tool in developing a positive mindset. Taking time each day to reflect on what we are grateful for helps shift our focus from what's lacking to what we have. It allows us to appreciate the present moment and fosters a sense of contentment and optimism. Gratitude helps us maintain perspective and stay motivated on our journey of self-discipline.

In conclusion, cultivating a positive and growth-oriented mindset is instrumental in transforming our habits and mindset. By believing in ourselves, embracing challenges, and seeking growth opportunities, we can unlock our full potential. Surrounding ourselves with positive influences and practicing gratitude further strengthens our mindset. With a positive and growth-oriented mindset, we can overcome obstacles, achieve our goals, and lead a fulfilling and successful life.

In today's fast-paced and competitive world, cultivating a positive and growth-oriented mindset is essential for achieving success and personal fulfillment. The power of self-discipline plays a crucial role in transforming your habits and mindset to achieve your goals. This subchapter will delve into the importance of adopting a positive mindset and provide practical tips for cultivating it.

A positive mindset is a state of mind that focuses on possibilities, growth, and learning from setbacks. It involves shifting your perspective from a fixed mindset, where you believe your abilities are limited, to a growth mindset, where you believe in your potential to improve through effort and perseverance.

One key aspect of cultivating a positive mindset is developing self-awareness. By understanding your thoughts, beliefs, and emotions, you can identify any negative patterns or self-limiting beliefs that might be holding you back. Through self-reflection and introspection, you can challenge and replace these negative beliefs with positive and empowering ones.

Another essential element in cultivating a positive mindset is practicing gratitude. Gratitude allows you to appreciate the present moment and focus on the positive aspects of your life. By regularly expressing gratitude for even the smallest things, you shift your focus from what is lacking to what you already have, fostering a sense of contentment and fulfillment.

Additionally, surrounding yourself with positive influences and like-minded individuals can significantly impact your mindset. Seek out supportive friends, mentors, or role models who embody the qualities and mindset you aspire to develop. Their positive energy, motivation, and encouragement will help you stay committed to your journey of self-discipline and personal growth.

Lastly, adopting a growth-oriented mindset means viewing challenges and failures as opportunities for learning and growth. Embrace setbacks as valuable lessons that provide you with the chance to improve and develop new skills. By reframing failures as stepping stones to success, you can foster resilience, persistence, and a belief in your ability to overcome obstacles.

In conclusion, cultivating a positive and growth-oriented mindset is a fundamental aspect of self-discipline. By developing self-awareness, practicing gratitude, surrounding yourself with positive influences, and embracing challenges, you can transform your habits and mindset, unlocking your full potential and achieving success in all areas of life. Remember, self-discipline is not just about willpower; it is about cultivating the right mindset to support your journey towards personal growth and fulfillment.

Chapter 9: Empowering Your Life with Self-Discipline

Improving Personal and Professional Relationships

In today's fast-paced world, where technology has made communication easier than ever, it is becoming increasingly important to focus on improving personal and professional relationships. Developing strong connections with others not only enhances our overall well-being but also plays a vital role in our success. This subchapter aims to provide valuable insights and practical strategies to help you nurture and strengthen your relationships.

One of the key factors in building successful relationships is self-discipline. By developing self-discipline, you can cultivate positive habits and mindset that will positively impact your interactions with others. Self-discipline allows you to control your emotions, listen actively, and respond thoughtfully, fostering open and effective communication.

To improve personal relationships, it is essential to prioritize quality time with loved ones. In our busy lives, it is easy to get caught up in work or other commitments, neglecting our closest relationships. By dedicating time and attention to our loved ones, we show them that they are a priority, which in turn strengthens the bond we share. Additionally, practicing empathy and understanding is crucial for maintaining healthy relationships. By putting ourselves in the shoes of others, we can better comprehend their feelings and perspectives, allowing us to build stronger connections.

In the professional realm, improving relationships with colleagues and superiors is vital for career growth and job satisfaction. Developing effective communication skills, such as active listening and assertiveness, is essential for building trust and respect in the workplace. By actively listening to others, you not only gain a better understanding of their needs and concerns but also demonstrate your commitment to collaboration and teamwork.

Furthermore, cultivating a positive and supportive work environment is crucial for fostering strong professional relationships. By providing constructive feedback, recognizing and appreciating the efforts of others, and offering assistance when needed, you contribute to a harmonious workplace where everyone feels valued and motivated.

In conclusion, improving personal and professional relationships is a fundamental aspect of our lives that requires self-discipline and conscious effort. By prioritizing quality time, practicing empathy, and developing effective communication skills, we can cultivate relationships that are fulfilling and contribute to our overall success and happiness. Whether in our personal or professional lives, the power of self-discipline can transform our habits and mindset, leading to stronger and more meaningful connections with others.

In today's fast-paced world, building and maintaining strong personal and professional relationships can greatly contribute to our overall happiness and success. Whether it is with our family, friends, colleagues, or clients, strong relationships are the backbone of a fulfilling life. By incorporating self-discipline into our interactions, we can enhance these relationships and foster a positive and supportive environment.

One of the key aspects of improving personal and professional relationships is effective communication. Many conflicts and misunderstandings arise from miscommunication or the lack of it. By practicing self-discipline in our conversations, we can learn to actively listen, express ourselves clearly, and respond thoughtfully. This requires being present in the moment, giving our undivided attention, and avoiding distractions. By doing so, we can foster trust, empathy, and understanding, ultimately strengthening our connections.

Another crucial component of building strong relationships is respect. Self-discipline helps us cultivate a mindset that values and acknowledges the worth of others. It allows us to treat everyone with kindness, empathy, and consideration, regardless of their background or opinions. By practicing self-discipline, we can refrain from engaging in negative behaviors such as gossiping, criticizing, or being judgmental, which can damage relationships. Instead, we can focus on finding common ground, appreciating differences, and fostering a supportive and inclusive atmosphere.

Furthermore, self-discipline plays a vital role in maintaining healthy boundaries within relationships. It empowers us to prioritize our needs while respecting the needs of others. By setting clear boundaries and communicating them assertively yet respectfully, we can avoid resentment, conflicts, and burnout. Self-discipline helps us say no when necessary, delegate tasks, and find a balance between our personal and professional commitments. This not only enhances our well-being but also demonstrates respect for ourselves and others.

Lastly, self-discipline enables us to continuously work on our personal growth and development, which positively impacts our relationships.

By taking responsibility for our actions, learning from our mistakes, and striving for self-improvement, we become better versions of ourselves. This inspires and uplifts those around us, creating a positive ripple effect in our personal and professional lives.

In conclusion, self-discipline is a fundamental tool for improving personal and professional relationships. By practicing effective communication, respect, setting healthy boundaries, and personal growth, we can enhance our connections with others. Whether it is with our loved ones or colleagues, the power of self-discipline can transform our relationships, leading to a more fulfilling and successful life for everyone.

In our journey towards self-discipline, it is crucial to recognize the significant impact our personal and professional relationships can have on our overall growth and success. Relationships play a pivotal role in our lives, shaping our mindset, habits, and ultimately, our level of self-discipline. Whether it be with family, friends, colleagues, or even acquaintances, fostering healthy and positive connections can greatly enhance our personal and professional lives.

One of the fundamental aspects of improving relationships is effective communication. Communication is not just about speaking; it involves active listening, empathy, and understanding. By developing our communication skills, we can build stronger connections with others, resolve conflicts, and avoid misunderstandings. This includes being mindful of our tone, body language, and choice of words.

Another vital aspect is cultivating empathy and compassion. Understanding and appreciating the perspectives, feelings, and needs of others helps us create a supportive environment. Empathy enables us to connect with others on a deeper level, fostering trust and building stronger bonds. By practicing compassion, we can provide emotional support and encouragement, helping others thrive and grow alongside us.

Additionally, setting boundaries is crucial to maintaining healthy relationships. It is essential to respect our own needs and limitations while also respecting those of others. By clearly communicating our boundaries, we can prevent resentment, misunderstandings, and burnout. This allows us to create harmonious relationships built on mutual respect and understanding.

Furthermore, practicing gratitude can significantly enhance our relationships. Expressing appreciation for the people in our lives not only strengthens our connections but also boosts our own well-being. Gratitude cultivates a positive mindset, promotes forgiveness, and encourages us to focus on the positive aspects of our relationships.

In the professional realm, building strong networks and alliances can open doors to opportunities and growth. By actively seeking out mentors and colleagues who inspire us, we can learn from their experiences and gain valuable insights. Collaboration and teamwork become easier when we surround ourselves with individuals who share our values and goals.

Improving personal and professional relationships is an ongoing process that requires self-awareness, patience, and effort. It is essential to continuously evaluate and reflect on our interactions, seeking opportunities for growth and improvement. By prioritizing the development of our relationships, we not only enhance our own self-discipline but also create a supportive network that propels us towards success in all areas of life.

Enhancing Productivity and Time Management Skills

Introduction:
In today's fast-paced world, where distractions are aplenty, enhancing productivity and time management skills has become more important than ever before. The ability to stay focused, manage time effectively, and accomplish tasks efficiently can be a game-changer in both personal and professional spheres. This subchapter aims to provide practical tips and strategies to help individuals develop and refine their productivity and time management skills, ultimately leading to a more disciplined and fulfilling life.

Understanding the Power of Self-Discipline:
Before delving into the specific techniques, it is vital to grasp the significance of self-discipline. Self-discipline is the foundation upon which productivity and time management skills are built. It is the ability to overcome procrastination, resist temptations, and stay committed to tasks at hand. By cultivating self-discipline, one can unlock the power to accomplish more in less time, paving the way for personal and professional success.

Setting Clear Goals and Priorities:
The first step in enhancing productivity and time management is setting clear goals and priorities. Without a defined destination, it becomes challenging to allocate time effectively. By identifying long-term goals and breaking them down into smaller, actionable tasks, individuals can stay focused and motivated. Prioritizing tasks based on their urgency and importance ensures that precious time is allocated to activities that truly matter.

Effective Planning and Time Blocking: Planning plays a crucial role in effective time management. By creating a well-structured schedule and blocking out specific time slots for various tasks, individuals can optimize their productivity. Time blocking involves dedicating uninterrupted periods to specific activities, eliminating distractions and allowing for deep focus. Additionally, leveraging productivity tools and techniques such as to-do lists, calendars, and digital apps can further streamline planning and organization.

Eliminating Time Wasters and Distractions: To maximize productivity, it is essential to identify and eliminate time wasters and distractions. These can include excessive social media usage, unnecessary meetings, multitasking, or disorganized workspaces. By consciously minimizing or eliminating these distractions, individuals can reclaim valuable time and channel their energy into meaningful tasks.

Utilizing Effective Time Management Techniques: Several time management techniques can significantly enhance productivity. These include the Pomodoro Technique, which involves working in focused bursts followed by short breaks, the Eisenhower Matrix for prioritization, and the 80/20 rule, which suggests that 80% of results come from 20% of efforts. By experimenting with different techniques and finding what works best, individuals can leverage their time effectively.

Conclusion:
Enhancing productivity and time management skills is not an overnight process; it requires consistent effort and self-discipline. By

setting clear goals, effective planning, eliminating distractions, and utilizing time management techniques, individuals can transform their habits and mindset, leading to increased productivity, reduced stress, and a more fulfilling life. Developing these skills is a lifelong journey, and the rewards are immeasurable. So, embrace the power of self-discipline and start your journey towards a more productive and balanced life today!

In today's fast-paced and ever-demanding world, it is crucial to possess effective productivity and time management skills. The ability to accomplish more in less time while maintaining focus and efficiency can make a significant difference in both personal and professional success. This subchapter explores various strategies and techniques to enhance productivity and improve time management skills, allowing individuals to harness the power of self-discipline.

One of the fundamental principles of productivity is understanding the importance of setting clear goals. Without a clear direction, it becomes easy to get overwhelmed and waste valuable time on unimportant tasks. By setting specific, measurable, attainable, relevant, and time-bound (SMART) goals, individuals can prioritize their activities and focus on what truly matters.

Another critical aspect of productivity is the ability to manage distractions effectively. In today's digital age, distractions are abundant, from social media notifications to constant email alerts. Learning to minimize these distractions and create a distraction-free environment is essential for maintaining focus and maximizing productivity. Techniques such as time blocking, where dedicated blocks of time are allocated to specific tasks, can help individuals stay on track and avoid getting sidetracked.

Moreover, effective time management involves understanding personal energy levels and peak productivity times. Each individual has their own unique energy patterns throughout the day, where they feel most energized and focused. Identifying these peak productivity times and scheduling important tasks during these periods can greatly enhance productivity and efficiency.

Furthermore, incorporating effective delegation and outsourcing strategies can significantly optimize time management. Recognizing that not every task requires personal attention and learning to delegate tasks to capable individuals can free up valuable time for more important responsibilities. Additionally, outsourcing non-essential tasks or seeking assistance where possible can further enhance productivity and allow individuals to focus on their core competencies.

Finally, it is vital to take breaks and practice self-care. Working tirelessly without breaks can lead to burnout and decreased productivity in the long run. By incorporating regular breaks, exercise, and relaxation techniques into daily routines, individuals can recharge their energy levels and maintain high productivity levels.

In conclusion, enhancing productivity and time management skills is crucial for anyone seeking personal and professional success. By setting clear goals, managing distractions, understanding personal energy patterns, delegating tasks, and practicing self-care, individuals can harness the power of self-discipline to accomplish more in less time. With dedication and consistent practice, these skills can be developed and become an integral part of one's daily routine, leading to increased productivity, improved outcomes, and ultimately, a more fulfilling and successful life.

In today's fast-paced world, the ability to enhance productivity and manage time effectively has become crucial for success in both personal and professional endeavors. In this subchapter, we will explore strategies and techniques that can help individuals develop their productivity and time management skills, ultimately leading to improved self-discipline and a transformed mindset.

One of the first steps towards enhancing productivity is to prioritize tasks. By identifying and focusing on high-priority activities, individuals can make the most out of their limited time and energy. This involves setting clear goals and breaking them down into smaller, more manageable tasks. Additionally, it is important to differentiate between urgent and important tasks, ensuring that the most critical ones are addressed first.

Another key aspect of productivity and time management is the ability to eliminate distractions. In today's digital age, it is easy to get sidetracked by social media, emails, and other non-essential activities. By implementing strategies such as time blocking, individuals can allocate specific time slots for focused work and minimize distractions. This may involve turning off notifications, creating a dedicated workspace, or using productivity apps and tools.

Furthermore, effective time management involves learning how to delegate tasks and ask for help when needed. Many individuals struggle with the misconception that they must handle everything themselves, leading to overwhelm and inefficiency. By recognizing one's strengths and weaknesses, individuals can leverage the skills and expertise of others, freeing up time for more important tasks.

In addition to these strategies, it is crucial to develop healthy habits and routines that support productivity. This includes practices such as regular exercise, proper nutrition, and adequate sleep. Taking care of one's physical and mental well-being is essential for maintaining focus and energy throughout the day.

Lastly, enhancing productivity and time management skills requires a commitment to self-discipline. This involves developing a mindset that values long-term goals over short-term gratification. By practicing self-control, individuals can avoid procrastination, stay focused on tasks at hand, and make consistent progress towards their objectives.

In conclusion, enhancing productivity and time management skills is essential for individuals seeking to improve their self-discipline and mindset. By prioritizing tasks, eliminating distractions, delegating when necessary, and cultivating healthy habits, individuals can maximize their productivity and make the most out of their time. Ultimately, mastering these skills will empower individuals to achieve their goals and lead a more fulfilled and successful life.

Achieving Personal Goals and Ambitions

Setting personal goals and ambitions is an essential step towards personal growth and success. Without clear objectives, we often find ourselves drifting through life, lacking direction and purpose. However, with the power of self-discipline, we can transform our habits and mindset to achieve our wildest dreams.

Self-discipline is the key ingredient to accomplishing personal goals and ambitions. It is the ability to control our impulses, stay focused, and persevere through challenges. By developing self-discipline, we can overcome procrastination, distractions, and self-doubt, enabling us to make consistent progress towards our aspirations.

The first step towards achieving personal goals is to dcfinc thcm clearly. Without a clear vision, we are merely wandering aimlessly. Take the time to reflect on what truly matters to you, both in the short and long term. Set specific, measurable, attainable, relevant, and time-bound (SMART) goals that align with your values and passions.

Once you have set your goals, it is crucial to create a plan of action. Break your goals down into smaller, manageable tasks that you can tackle one step at a time. This not only makes the journey less overwhelming but also allows you to track your progress and celebrate small victories along the way.

Self-discipline requires consistency and commitment. It is essential to develop healthy habits and routines that support your goals. Eliminate distractions and create an environment conducive to productivity. Surround yourself with like-minded individuals who inspire and motivate you to stay focused on your path.

However, self-discipline is not about being rigid or punishing yourself for mistakes. It is about cultivating self-awareness and self-control. Understand that setbacks and failures are a natural part of the journey. Learn from them, adjust your approach if needed, and keep moving forward with determination and resilience.

To maintain self-discipline, it is vital to stay motivated. Regularly remind yourself of the reasons why you set your goals in the first place. Visualize the future you desire and the person you aspire to become. Celebrate your progress and reward yourself for your efforts, but also hold yourself accountable for your actions.

In conclusion, achieving personal goals and ambitions is within reach for everyone through the power of self-discipline. By setting clear goals, creating a plan of action, developing healthy habits, and staying motivated, we can transform our lives and accomplish what we once thought was impossible. Embrace self-discipline, and watch as your dreams become a reality.

In today's fast-paced and competitive world, it is crucial to have a clear understanding of our personal goals and ambitions. Without a defined direction, we may find ourselves drifting through life, lacking fulfillment and purpose. However, with the power of self-discipline, we can transform our habits and mindset, enabling us to achieve our personal goals and ambitions.

Self-discipline is the key ingredient to success in any area of life. It is the ability to control our impulses, emotions, and desires in pursuit of a higher purpose. By harnessing the power of self-discipline, we can overcome obstacles, develop new habits, and make consistent progress towards our goals.

The first step towards achieving personal goals and ambitions is to set clear and specific objectives. It is essential to define what we want to achieve and establish a timeline for accomplishing it. This clarity helps us stay focused and motivated, even when faced with challenges along the way.

Once we have set our goals, it is important to develop a plan of action. This plan should break down our goals into smaller, manageable tasks. By taking small steps consistently, we create momentum and build confidence in our ability to achieve what we set out to do.

Self-discipline plays a vital role in following through with our plans. It requires us to prioritize our actions and resist the temptation of immediate gratification. This means saying no to distractions, overcoming procrastination, and staying committed to the tasks at hand.

To cultivate self-discipline, we must also develop healthy habits. Habits are powerful forces that can either propel us towards success or hinder our progress. By consciously choosing positive habits that align with our goals, we create a strong foundation for self-discipline to thrive.

It is important to acknowledge that achieving personal goals and ambitions requires effort and perseverance. There will be times when we encounter setbacks and face obstacles. However, with self-discipline, we can learn from these experiences, adapt our approach, and continue moving forward.

In conclusion, self-discipline is the driving force behind achieving personal goals and ambitions. By setting clear objectives, developing a plan of action, and cultivating healthy habits, we empower ourselves to make consistent progress towards our desired outcomes. With self-discipline, we can transform our habits and mindset, unlocking our true potential and living a life of purpose and fulfillment.

Setting personal goals and ambitions is a crucial step towards leading a fulfilling and successful life. However, the journey towards accomplishing these aspirations requires self-discipline – the key ingredient that propels individuals towards their desired destination. In this subchapter, we will explore the significance of self-discipline in achieving personal goals and ambitions, and uncover effective strategies to cultivate and strengthen this essential trait.

Self-discipline serves as the driving force behind turning dreams into reality. It empowers individuals to overcome obstacles, resist temptations, and stay focused on their objectives, even when faced with adversity. Without self-discipline, ambitions can remain mere fantasies, forever out of reach. Therefore, it is essential to embrace self-discipline as a fundamental pillar of personal growth and achievement.

To cultivate self-discipline, it is important to start by setting clear and specific goals. Vague aspirations are difficult to pursue, as they lack a defined path. By setting concrete goals, individuals can create a roadmap and break down their ambitions into manageable steps. This not only makes the journey towards achievement more attainable but also provides a sense of direction and purpose.

Moreover, it is crucial to develop effective habits and routines that support personal goals. Habits are powerful drivers of behavior, and by consciously establishing positive habits, individuals can ensure consistent progress towards their ambitions. For instance, if the goal is to become a published author, setting a routine of writing for a specific amount of time each day can significantly contribute to the realization of this ambition.

Self-discipline also involves managing time and resources efficiently. Prioritizing tasks, avoiding distractions, and staying organized are vital components of effective time management. By allocating time wisely and dedicating focused energy to each task, individuals can optimize their productivity and inch closer to their desired outcomes.

Furthermore, self-discipline thrives on resilience and perseverance. In the face of setbacks and failures, it is crucial to remain determined and continue the pursuit of personal goals. Setbacks should be seen as learning opportunities rather than roadblocks, as they provide valuable insights and help refine strategies.

In conclusion, achieving personal goals and ambitions requires self-discipline. It is the force that empowers individuals to stay focused, overcome challenges, and turn dreams into reality. By setting clear goals, developing positive habits, managing time efficiently, and embracing resilience, individuals can strengthen their self-discipline and embark on a transformative journey of personal growth and achievement. Remember, self-discipline is not a trait reserved for a select few; it is a skill that can be cultivated and mastered by anyone willing to put in the effort.

Cultivating Happiness and Fulfillment

In our pursuit of a successful and meaningful life, happiness and fulfillment often take center stage. We all desire to experience joy, contentment, and a sense of purpose. However, achieving and maintaining these states requires more than just luck or circumstance; it requires the cultivation of self-discipline.

Self-discipline is the foundation upon which happiness and fulfillment are built. It is the ability to control our thoughts, emotions, and actions to align them with our long-term goals and values. By practicing self-discipline, we can create habits and mindsets that lead to a more fulfilling life.

One crucial aspect of cultivating happiness and fulfillment is setting meaningful goals. When we have a clear vision of what we want to achieve, we can direct our efforts towards it, creating a sense of purpose and motivation. Self-discipline allows us to stay focused on our goals, even when faced with challenges or distractions. It helps us overcome procrastination and persevere through difficulties, leading us closer to our desired outcomes.

Another key element in cultivating happiness and fulfillment is taking care of our physical and mental well-being. Self-discipline enables us to make healthy choices, such as exercising regularly, eating nutritious food, and getting enough rest. By prioritizing self-care, we improve our energy levels, mood, and overall quality of life. Additionally, practicing self-discipline in managing our thoughts and emotions helps us develop resilience and emotional intelligence, enabling us to navigate life's ups and downs with grace and composure.

Moreover, cultivating gratitude and practicing mindfulness are essential components of happiness and fulfillment. Self-discipline allows us to train our minds to focus on the present moment, appreciating the beauty and blessings in our lives. By practicing gratitude, we shift our perspectives and become more aware of the positive aspects of our existence. This mindset not only enhances our own well-being but also strengthens our relationships and interactions with others.

In conclusion, cultivating happiness and fulfillment requires the power of self-discipline. By setting meaningful goals, taking care of our physical and mental well-being, and practicing gratitude and mindfulness, we can transform our habits and mindset to create a more fulfilling life. Self-discipline empowers us to make choices that align with our values, overcome obstacles, and live a life of purpose and joy. So, let us embrace the power of self-discipline and embark on a journey towards a happier and more fulfilled existence.

In today's fast-paced world, where productivity and achievement are often prioritized, it is easy to overlook the importance of cultivating happiness and fulfillment in our lives. However, true self-discipline involves not only achieving goals but also finding joy and contentment along the way. In this subchapter, we will explore how to cultivate happiness and fulfillment through the power of self-discipline.

One of the first steps in cultivating happiness is to establish a clear vision of what it means to be fulfilled. Take some time to reflect on your values, passions, and purpose in life. What brings you joy? What activities make you feel fulfilled? By understanding what truly matters to you, you can align your actions and goals with your inner desires, leading to a greater sense of purpose and happiness.

Another key aspect of cultivating happiness is practicing gratitude. It is all too easy to focus on what we lack or what is not going right in our lives. However, by shifting our attention to the positive aspects, we can foster a mindset of gratitude. Take a few moments each day to identify three things you are grateful for. This simple practice can rewire your brain to focus on the abundance and blessings in your life, leading to increased happiness and fulfillment.

Self-care is another essential component of cultivating happiness. It is important to prioritize your physical, mental, and emotional well-being. Engage in activities that bring you joy and rejuvenate your spirit. Whether it's taking a walk in nature, practicing mindfulness and meditation, or indulging in a hobby you love, investing time in self-care allows you to recharge, reduce stress, and find happiness in the present moment.

Furthermore, cultivating healthy relationships is crucial for long-lasting happiness and fulfillment. Surround yourself with people who uplift and inspire you. Nurture meaningful connections and invest time and effort in building and maintaining strong relationships. By fostering positive and supportive relationships, you will create a sense of belonging, love, and happiness in your life.

Lastly, remember that happiness and fulfillment are not destinations; they are ongoing journeys. Embrace the process and be patient with yourself. Self-discipline involves consistent effort and practice. Celebrate small victories and learn from setbacks. By cultivating happiness and fulfillment through self-discipline, you can create a life that is not only successful but also deeply satisfying and joyful.

In conclusion, cultivating happiness and fulfillment is an integral part of self-discipline. By aligning your actions with your values, practicing gratitude, prioritizing self-care, nurturing relationships, and embracing the journey, you can experience a profound sense of happiness and fulfillment. Remember, true self-discipline encompasses not only achieving external goals but also finding inner contentment and joy. Start today, and embark on a path that leads you to a life filled with happiness and fulfillment.

In our quest for success and personal growth, one crucial aspect that we often overlook is cultivating happiness and fulfillment. While self-discipline is essential for achieving our goals, true happiness and fulfillment come from within. In this subchapter, we will explore the transformative power of self-discipline in cultivating lasting happiness and fulfillment in our lives.

Many people mistakenly believe that external achievements and possessions will bring them happiness. However, true happiness lies in aligning our actions and values with our authentic selves. Self-discipline plays a vital role in this process as it enables us to make choices that are in line with our long-term happiness and fulfillment.

One of the key principles of cultivating happiness and fulfillment is finding purpose and meaning in our lives. Self-discipline empowers us to set clear goals and work towards them with determination and perseverance. By aligning our actions with our values and purpose, we can derive a sense of fulfillment from every step we take towards our goals.

Another crucial aspect of cultivating happiness and fulfillment is practicing gratitude and mindfulness. Self-discipline helps us develop the habit of gratitude, enabling us to appreciate the present moment and find joy in even the smallest of things. By practicing mindfulness, we become more aware of our thoughts and emotions, allowing us to make conscious choices that contribute to our overall well-being.

Furthermore, self-discipline helps us develop and maintain healthy habits that promote happiness and fulfillment. Whether it is regular exercise, a nutritious diet, or spending quality time with loved ones, self-discipline allows us to prioritize activities that nourish our mind, body, and soul. By consistently engaging in these activities, we create a positive cycle that enhances our overall happiness and fulfillment.

Lastly, self-discipline empowers us to overcome challenges and setbacks that come our way. It equips us with the resilience and determination needed to bounce back from failures and continue on our path towards happiness and fulfillment. By viewing setbacks as opportunities for growth and learning, we can maintain a positive mindset and keep moving forward.

In conclusion, cultivating happiness and fulfillment is an essential aspect of our personal growth journey. Self-discipline acts as a guiding force, helping us align our actions with our values, find purpose and meaning, practice gratitude and mindfulness, develop healthy habits, and overcome challenges. By embracing self-discipline, we can transform our habits and mindset to create a life filled with lasting happiness and fulfillment. So, let us embark on this journey of self-discovery and self-discipline, and unlock the power to cultivate true happiness and fulfillment in our lives.

Chapter 10: Maintaining Self-Discipline Beyond the Book

Integrating Self-Discipline into Daily Life

Self-discipline is the key to achieving success, happiness, and personal growth in every aspect of life. It is the ability to control your thoughts, emotions, and actions to align them with your long-term goals. While self-discipline may seem challenging, it is a skill that can be learned and practiced by anyone willing to put in the effort. In this subchapter, we will explore various strategies to integrate self-discipline into your daily life.

One of the first steps to developing self-discipline is to identify your core values and set clear goals. Understanding what truly matters to you will provide the motivation and direction needed to stay focused and disciplined. Write down your goals, both short-term and long-term, and create a plan to achieve them. Break these goals into smaller, actionable steps that you can work on daily.

Another crucial aspect of self-discipline is managing your time effectively. Time is a precious resource, and disciplined individuals recognize the importance of utilizing it wisely. Prioritize tasks based on their significance and urgency. Eliminate distractions, such as social media or excessive television, and create a schedule that allows dedicated time for work, personal growth, and relaxation.

Developing healthy habits is another way to integrate self-discipline into your daily life. Start with small changes, such as waking up early, exercising regularly, or practicing mindfulness. Consistency is key when it comes to building habits, so commit to making these changes a part of your routine. Over time, these habits will become second nature, and you will find it easier to stay disciplined in other areas of your life as well.

Self-discipline also involves taking care of your physical and mental well-being. Get enough sleep, eat nutritious meals, and engage in activities that bring you joy and relaxation. Prioritizing self-care will provide you with the energy and mental clarity needed to face challenges and make disciplined choices.

Remember, self-discipline is a journey, and it requires patience and self-compassion. It is okay to make mistakes along the way, as long as you learn from them and keep pushing forward. Surround yourself with supportive individuals who share your values and goals, as they can provide encouragement and accountability.

By integrating self-discipline into your daily life, you will experience an incredible transformation. You will become more focused, confident, and resilient in pursuing your dreams. Embrace the power of self-discipline, and unlock your full potential.

Self-discipline is a powerful tool that can help us transform our habits and mindset, leading to personal growth and success in all areas of life. Whether you want to improve your health, achieve your career goals, or enhance your relationships, self-discipline is the key to unlocking your true potential.

In this subchapter, we will explore practical ways to integrate self-discipline into your daily life. By adopting these strategies, you can develop the necessary mindset and habits to cultivate self-discipline and achieve lasting results.

1.   Set   Clear   Goals:
Start by defining your goals. What do you want to accomplish? By setting clear, specific, and measurable objectives, you give yourself a target to aim for. This clarity will help you stay focused and committed to your journey.

2.   Create   a   Routine:
Establishing a daily routine can provide structure and consistency, making it easier to practice self-discipline. Designate specific times for activities such as exercise, work, and leisure, and stick to your schedule as much as possible. Consistency breeds self-discipline.

3.   Prioritize   Tasks:
Learn to prioritize your tasks based on their importance and urgency. By tackling the most critical tasks first, you avoid procrastination and develop the discipline to take action promptly.

4.   Practice   Time   Management:
Effective time management is crucial for self-discipline. Set realistic deadlines for tasks, avoid distractions, and allocate your time wisely. By managing your time effectively, you ensure that you have ample space in your schedule to work towards your goals.

5.   Embrace   Delayed   Gratification:
Self-discipline often requires sacrificing short-term pleasures for long-term gains. Learn to delay gratification by resisting temptations that hinder your progress. Remind yourself of the bigger picture and the rewards that await you in the future.

6.   Cultivate   a   Growth   Mindset: Adopting a growth mindset is essential for developing self-discipline. Believe in your ability to change and grow, even when faced with setbacks or challenges. Embrace failures as learning opportunities and keep striving towards improvement.

7.   Seek   Accountability   and   Support: Enlist the support of friends, family, or a mentor who can hold you accountable for your actions. Share your goals with them and ask for their guidance and encouragement. Having someone to answer to can greatly enhance your self-discipline.

Remember, self-discipline is a skill that can be learned and improved upon. By integrating these strategies into your daily life, you will gradually develop the discipline to overcome obstacles, persevere through challenges, and achieve your desired outcomes. Start today and unlock the power of self-discipline to transform your life.

Self-discipline is a powerful tool that can transform your habits and mindset, leading you towards a more fulfilling and successful life. It is a skill that everyone can cultivate, regardless of age, background, or profession. By incorporating self-discipline into your daily routine, you can achieve personal growth, accomplish your goals, and overcome obstacles that may be holding you back.

Creating a strong foundation for self-discipline starts with understanding the importance of setting clear goals. When you have well-defined objectives, you can align your actions and decisions accordingly. Begin by identifying what you truly want to achieve, whether it's in your career, relationships, health, or personal development. Break down these goals into smaller, manageable steps, and create a roadmap to guide your progress.

One of the key aspects of self-discipline is the ability to manage your time effectively. Time management involves prioritizing tasks, organizing your schedule, and eliminating distractions. By practicing techniques such as creating to-do lists, setting deadlines, and avoiding procrastination, you can optimize your productivity and make the most of your day.

Another crucial component of self-discipline is developing healthy habits. Start by examining your current habits and identifying any negative patterns that may be hindering your progress. Replace these habits with positive ones that align with your goals. For example, if you want to improve your physical fitness, establish a daily exercise routine and stick to it consistently. Remember that self-discipline is not about denying yourself pleasure or enjoyment, but rather, about making conscious choices that support your long-term goals.

Incorporating self-discipline into daily life also requires cultivating a growth mindset. Embrace challenges as opportunities for growth and view setbacks as learning experiences. By adopting a positive outlook and believing in your ability to improve, you can overcome obstacles and persevere through difficult times.

To maintain self-discipline, it is important to stay motivated and hold yourself accountable. Find sources of inspiration that resonate with you, whether it's reading books, listening to podcasts, or surrounding yourself with like-minded individuals. Additionally, establish systems of accountability, such as sharing your goals with a trusted friend or using technology to track your progress.

Integrating self-discipline into your daily life can be challenging, but the rewards are immeasurable. By consistently practicing self-discipline, you will develop resilience, improve your focus, and unlock your full potential. Remember, self-discipline is not a one-time achievement, but an ongoing journey towards personal growth and fulfillment. Start today, and witness the transformative power of self-discipline in your life.

Seeking Continuous Growth and Development

In today's fast-paced world, where change is the only constant, it has become imperative for every individual to seek continuous growth and development. The ability to adapt, learn, and evolve is crucial, especially in the realm of self-discipline. "The Power of Self-Discipline: Transforming Your Habits and Mindset" is a book that recognizes the significance of continuous growth and offers valuable insights and strategies for achieving personal development.

Self-discipline, as a niche, encompasses a wide range of individuals from all walks of life. Whether you are a student striving to excel academically, a professional aiming for career advancement, or simply an individual looking to improve your personal habits, this subchapter is tailored to address your needs.

The subchapter "Seeking Continuous Growth and Development" delves deep into the importance of embracing change and adopting a growth mindset. It emphasizes the idea that self-discipline is not a fixed trait but a skill that can be cultivated and enhanced over time. By adopting this mindset, individuals can break free from limiting beliefs and overcome obstacles that hinder their personal growth.

The content of this subchapter revolves around providing practical strategies and actionable steps to facilitate continuous growth. It unravels the significance of setting goals, creating effective habits, and implementing self-reflection practices. Moreover, it emphasizes the importance of seeking knowledge, learning from experiences, and embracing new opportunities.

Furthermore, the subchapter addresses the challenges individuals may encounter during their growth journey. It explores common obstacles such as fear of failure, self-doubt, and resistance to change. By providing guidance and practical advice, it empowers readers to overcome these obstacles and stay committed to their growth and development.

The subchapter also highlights the importance of seeking support and accountability. It acknowledges that personal growth is not a solitary journey and encourages readers to build a network of like-minded individuals who can provide guidance, motivation, and constructive feedback.

In conclusion, "Seeking Continuous Growth and Development" is a subchapter within "The Power of Self-Discipline: Transforming Your Habits and Mindset" that caters to individuals from various backgrounds. It offers practical strategies, actionable steps, and guidance to help readers embrace change, adopt a growth mindset, and achieve personal development. By delving into the challenges and providing solutions, this subchapter empowers readers to overcome obstacles and embark on a continuous journey of growth and self-discipline.

In the journey of life, seeking continuous growth and development is a fundamental aspect of personal and professional success. The ability to adapt, learn, and evolve is crucial in today's rapidly changing world. This subchapter aims to provide insights and strategies to cultivate self-discipline and embrace a mindset of continuous growth and development.

Self-discipline forms the foundation for personal growth. It is the ability to control and direct our thoughts, actions, and emotions towards achieving our goals. Without self-discipline, our desires and aspirations remain mere dreams. However, by cultivating self-discipline, we can transform our habits and mindset, unlocking our full potential.

The first step towards continuous growth and development is to set clear and realistic goals. By defining our objectives, we gain clarity on what we want to achieve and can create a roadmap to reach our destination. Setting goals also helps us stay focused and motivated, ensuring that we make progress consistently.

To maintain self-discipline and sustain growth, it is crucial to develop effective habits. Habits are powerful tools that shape our lives. By consciously cultivating positive habits and eliminating negative ones, we can create a strong foundation for continuous growth. Regular exercise, reading, and practicing mindfulness are examples of habits that contribute to personal development.

Embracing a growth mindset is another essential aspect of seeking continuous growth and development. A growth mindset is the belief that our abilities and intelligence can be developed through dedication and hard work. By adopting this mindset, we become open to challenges, view failures as learning opportunities, and constantly seek ways to improve ourselves.

Continuous learning is a key component of growth and development. It expands our knowledge, enhances our skills, and broadens our perspectives. Engaging in lifelong learning through reading, attending seminars, and seeking mentorship enables us to stay relevant in an ever-changing world. It also fosters creativity and innovation, allowing us to explore new possibilities and seize opportunities.

Finally, seeking continuous growth and development requires perseverance and resilience. It is essential to stay committed to our goals, even in the face of obstacles and setbacks. By maintaining a positive attitude and learning from failures, we can turn challenges into stepping stones towards growth.

In conclusion, seeking continuous growth and development is a lifelong journey that requires self-discipline, a growth mindset, effective habits, and a commitment to learning. By embracing these principles, we can unlock our full potential, achieve personal and professional success, and lead fulfilling lives. Remember, the power of self-discipline lies within each of us; it is up to us to harness it and transform our habits and mindset for continuous growth and development.

In our journey towards personal growth and self-improvement, seeking continuous growth and development is crucial. It is through this process that we can unlock our true potential, transform our habits, and adopt a mindset that propels us towards success. This subchapter will explore the importance of constant growth and development in the realm of self-discipline, providing insights and strategies that can be applied by individuals from all walks of life.

Self-discipline is the foundation upon which all achievements are built. It is the ability to stay focused, motivated, and committed to our goals, even in the face of challenges and obstacles. However, self-discipline is not a fixed trait, but rather a skill that can be developed and strengthened over time. To truly master self-discipline, we must embrace the concept of continuous growth and development.

One key aspect of seeking continuous growth is the willingness to step outside of our comfort zones. Growth occurs when we challenge ourselves and push beyond our limits. By constantly seeking new experiences, learning opportunities, and setting ambitious goals, we create an environment that fosters personal development. This process allows us to expand our knowledge, skills, and abilities, ultimately enhancing our self-discipline.

Another important element of continuous growth and development is the cultivation of a growth mindset. This mindset embraces the belief that our abilities and intelligence can be developed through dedication and hard work. By adopting a growth mindset, we shift our focus from the fear of failure to the pursuit of growth and improvement. This positive mindset enables us to persevere through setbacks, learn from mistakes, and continuously develop our self-discipline.

To support our journey of continuous growth and development, it is essential to establish effective habits and routines. These habits act as the building blocks of self-discipline. By incorporating daily rituals such as goal setting, time management, and self-reflection, we create a structure that promotes consistent growth and development. Moreover, seeking feedback from mentors, coaches, or trusted individuals can provide valuable insights and guidance on areas where we can improve and refine our self-discipline.

In conclusion, seeking continuous growth and development is paramount in the realm of self-discipline. By embracing new challenges, cultivating a growth mindset, and establishing effective habits, we can transform our lives and unlock our true potential. Remember, self-discipline is not a destination but a lifelong journey, and by committing to constant growth and development, we can achieve remarkable feats and create a life of success and fulfillment.

Joining Supportive Communities and Networks

In our journey towards self-discipline, one of the most powerful tools at our disposal is the support and encouragement we receive from others. Joining supportive communities and networks can greatly enhance our ability to transform our habits and mindset. Regardless of your background or the specific areas in which you seek self-discipline, there is a community out there waiting to welcome you with open arms.

When we surround ourselves with like-minded individuals who are also striving for self-discipline, we create an environment conducive to growth and progress. These communities provide a space where we can share our struggles, successes, and experiences, fostering a sense of camaraderie and understanding. Through this mutual support, we gain motivation and accountability, pushing us to stay committed to our goals.

The beauty of joining supportive communities and networks is that they come in various forms. Whether it is an online forum, a local meetup group, or even a mentorship program, the options are endless. The internet, in particular, has made it easier than ever to connect with people who share our interests and aspirations. From social media groups to specialized forums, these virtual communities offer a platform to exchange ideas, seek advice, and find inspiration.

Being part of a supportive network not only provides emotional support but also opens doors to new opportunities. Through networking, we can connect with individuals who have already achieved the level of self-discipline we aspire to. Their wisdom and guidance can prove invaluable, helping us avoid common pitfalls and shortcuts on our journey towards self-discipline. Additionally, these connections may lead to collaborations, partnerships, or mentorship opportunities, further propelling our growth and development.

In joining supportive communities and networks, it is essential to actively participate and contribute. By sharing our own experiences and insights, we not only help others but also solidify our own understanding and commitment to self-discipline. Furthermore, engaging with a diverse group of individuals allows us to gain new perspectives and learn from different approaches. This collective wisdom strengthens our resolve and broadens our horizons, enabling us to tackle challenges with renewed vigor.

In conclusion, joining supportive communities and networks is a crucial step in harnessing the power of self-discipline. By surrounding ourselves with like-minded individuals, we create an environment that fosters growth, motivation, and accountability. Through these connections, we gain emotional support, access to valuable resources, and opportunities for collaboration. The journey towards self-discipline becomes less daunting when we realize that we are not alone and that there are countless others who are on a similar path. So, take the leap and find your tribe – together, we can transform our habits and mindset for a more disciplined and fulfilling life.

One of the most valuable resources in the journey of self-discipline is the support and encouragement of like-minded individuals. In a world where distractions and temptations are abundant, being part of a supportive community or network can make all the difference in staying focused and achieving your goals. Whether you are striving to develop self-discipline in your personal life, career, relationships, or health, joining these communities can provide the necessary tools and motivation to transform your habits and mindset.

Supportive communities and networks offer a unique environment where individuals can connect, share experiences, and learn from one another's successes and challenges. They provide a safe space where you can openly discuss your aspirations and struggles without fear of judgment. Surrounding yourself with people who are also committed to self-discipline will inspire you to push beyond your limits and strive for excellence.

These communities and networks come in various forms. Online forums, social media groups, workshops, and local meetups are just a few examples of platforms that facilitate connections among individuals on the same self-discipline journey. No matter your location or schedule, there are options available that suit your needs and preferences.

By joining these communities, you gain access to a wealth of knowledge and resources. Members often share practical tips, techniques, and strategies for overcoming obstacles and staying on track. They can recommend books, podcasts, or workshops that have helped them in their own self-discipline journey. Engaging with these resources not only expands your knowledge but also keeps you motivated and focused on your goals.

Furthermore, being part of a supportive community provides a sense of accountability. When you publicly declare your goals and progress, you are more likely to follow through and stay committed. The encouragement and support from fellow members will keep you motivated during tough times and celebrate your victories along the way.

Remember, self-discipline is not a solitary endeavor. By joining supportive communities and networks, you surround yourself with individuals who understand the challenges and rewards of self-discipline. Together, you can inspire and uplift each other, creating an environment that fosters personal growth and transformation.

Whether you are just starting your self-discipline journey or looking to take it to the next level, joining supportive communities and networks is a powerful step towards achieving your goals. Embrace the power of connection and collaboration, and watch as your self-discipline flourishes, transforming your habits and mindset.

One of the most effective ways to cultivate self-discipline and transform your habits and mindset is by joining supportive communities and networks. Surrounding yourself with like-minded individuals who are also committed to personal growth and self-discipline can significantly enhance your journey towards self-improvement.

Supportive communities and networks provide a nurturing environment where you can learn, grow, and receive encouragement from others who share similar goals and challenges. They can offer valuable insights, strategies, and resources that can accelerate your progress and help you overcome obstacles along the way.

One of the key benefits of joining supportive communities is the accountability they provide. When you make a commitment to your personal growth within a community, you are more likely to stay on track and follow through with your goals. The mutual support and encouragement from fellow members can serve as a powerful motivator, pushing you to strive for excellence and maintain your self-discipline even when faced with adversity or temptation.

Additionally, being part of a supportive community allows you to tap into a collective wisdom. You can leverage the experiences and knowledge of others who have already achieved what you are striving for. By learning from their successes and failures, you can gain valuable insights and avoid common pitfalls, saving yourself time and effort.

Supportive networks can also serve as a source of inspiration and motivation. Seeing others who have successfully transformed their habits and mindset can ignite a fire within you, fueling your determination to achieve similar results. Surrounding yourself with individuals who have a strong sense of self-discipline can help you raise your standards and push past your self-imposed limits.

In today's digital age, joining supportive communities and networks has become more accessible than ever. Online platforms and social media groups provide virtual spaces where you can connect with individuals who share your interests and goals, regardless of geographical limitations. These communities often host discussions, share resources, and offer support, allowing you to engage and participate at your own convenience.

In conclusion, joining supportive communities and networks is an invaluable strategy for enhancing your self-discipline and personal growth. By surrounding yourself with like-minded individuals who are also committed to self-improvement, you can benefit from accountability, collective wisdom, inspiration, and motivation. Whether you choose to join a local group or an online community, the support and encouragement you receive will undoubtedly propel you towards transforming your habits and mindset, ultimately leading to a more disciplined and fulfilling life.

Inspiring Others through Your Self-Discipline Journey

Self-discipline is a powerful tool that can transform our lives in ways we may never have imagined. It helps us develop habits that lead to success, productivity, and personal growth. However, self-discipline doesn't only benefit us; it also has the potential to inspire those around us. By sharing our self-discipline journey, we can motivate others to embark on their own path of self-improvement and achieve their goals.

When we demonstrate self-discipline, we become living examples of what is possible. People around us take notice and are inspired by the changes they see in our lives. Our determination, consistency, and resilience become a source of inspiration for others who may be struggling with their own discipline. They see that if we can do it, so can they.

One of the most effective ways to inspire others is through storytelling. By sharing our personal experiences, challenges, and triumphs, we can connect with people on a deeper level. We can relate to their struggles, validate their feelings, and offer guidance and support. Through our stories, we can show them that self-discipline is not a superpower reserved for a select few, but a skill that can be learned and cultivated by anyone.

It is important to be honest and transparent about our journey. We should not shy away from sharing our failures and setbacks because they are a natural part of the process. By being vulnerable, we let others know that it's okay to stumble and make mistakes along the way. It's about getting back up and continuing the journey that matters.

In addition to storytelling, we can also inspire others by providing practical tips and strategies for developing self-discipline. We can share the techniques that have worked for us, such as setting clear goals, creating routines, and practicing mindfulness. By offering these tools, we empower others to take control of their lives and make positive changes.

Finally, by supporting and encouraging others on their self-discipline journey, we create a community of like-minded individuals who can uplift and motivate one another. We can offer accountability partnerships, share resources, and celebrate each other's successes. Together, we can create a ripple effect of self-discipline and inspire even more people to transform their habits and mindset.

In conclusion, by sharing our self-discipline journey, we have the power to inspire others to embark on their own path of self-improvement. Through storytelling, practical tips, and building a supportive community, we can motivate and empower others to develop the self-discipline they need to achieve their goals. Remember, your journey is not just about you; it has the potential to impact the lives of countless individuals who are waiting to be inspired.

Self-discipline is a powerful force that can transform not only your own life but also the lives of those around you. When you embark on a journey of self-discipline, you become an inspiration to others, showing them what is possible when one commits to personal growth and development.

One of the most effective ways to inspire others through your self-discipline journey is by leading by example. People are more likely to be motivated and inspired when they see someone who is practicing what they preach. When you consistently demonstrate self-discipline in your daily life, others will take notice and be inspired to follow suit.

Sharing your story is another powerful way to inspire others. By sharing your own struggles, triumphs, and the lessons you have learned along the way, you can provide hope and motivation to those who may be facing similar challenges. When people see that you have overcome obstacles and achieved success through self-discipline, they will be encouraged to do the same.

Furthermore, it is important to be authentic and transparent in your journey. Nobody is perfect, and showing vulnerability can make your story relatable and resonate with others. By acknowledging your own mistakes and setbacks, you demonstrate that self-discipline is a lifelong journey, and that it is okay to stumble along the way. This can be incredibly inspiring for those who may be struggling with their own self-discipline efforts.

Another effective method to inspire others is by offering guidance and support. As you progress on your self-discipline journey, you will acquire valuable knowledge and skills that can benefit others. Share your insights, strategies, and tips with those who are seeking to develop self-discipline. By providing guidance and support, you empower others to take control of their lives and achieve their goals.

Lastly, celebrate the successes of others. When you see someone else making progress on their self-discipline journey, acknowledge and celebrate their achievements. By doing so, you create a positive and supportive environment that encourages others to continue their efforts.

In conclusion, inspiring others through your self-discipline journey is a powerful way to make a positive impact on the lives of those around you. By leading by example, sharing your story, being authentic, offering guidance, and celebrating the successes of others, you can motivate and encourage others to embrace self-discipline and transform their own lives. Remember, your self-discipline journey is not only about personal growth but also about inspiring and uplifting others on their own path to success.

Self-discipline is a powerful tool that can transform not only your own life but also inspire those around you. When you embark on a journey of self-discipline, you become a living example of what is possible when one commits to personal growth and development. Your actions speak louder than words, and by demonstrating your commitment to self-discipline, you can inspire others to do the same.

One of the most compelling aspects of self-discipline is its universal appeal. It is relevant to every individual, regardless of their background, age, or goals. Whether someone aspires to achieve financial success, improve their health, or enhance their relationships, self-discipline is the cornerstone of achieving those dreams. By sharing your own self-discipline journey, you can help others recognize the potential within themselves and inspire them to take action.

Your journey can serve as a powerful example of how self-discipline can overcome obstacles and setbacks. Life is filled with challenges, and it is through discipline that we can navigate these difficulties and continue moving forward. When others witness your determination and resilience, they are more likely to adopt a similar mindset and face their own challenges head-on.

Furthermore, your self-discipline journey can provide practical guidance and inspiration to those who may be struggling. As you share your strategies, techniques, and lessons learned, you empower others to make positive changes in their lives. Whether it is through setting goals, developing daily routines, or practicing self-care, your experiences can serve as a roadmap for others seeking self-discipline.

It is important to remember that inspiring others through your self-discipline journey is not about preaching or boasting about your accomplishments. Instead, it is about being authentic, vulnerable, and relatable. Share your failures as well as your successes, as they are both valuable learning experiences. By being open and honest, you create a safe space for others to connect with your journey and feel inspired to embark on their own path of self-discipline.

In conclusion, inspiring others through your self-discipline journey is a powerful way to impact lives and create a ripple effect of positive change. By sharing your story, demonstrating resilience, and offering practical guidance, you can motivate others to embrace self-discipline and transform their habits and mindset. Remember, your journey is not just about personal growth, but also about empowering others to unlock their full potential.